R0061768651

03/2012

D1490709

Linda Campanella offers her readers a wise, tender, and heartfelt account of her mother's last year of life and her family's participation in it. *When All That's Left of Me Is Love* is a brave and self-revealing gift from its author: one daughter's journey of hope and grief and deep, deep love for her mother.

Throughout the book Linda records exchanges, describes the events of the days and reveals the plots and plans to help her mother live to the fullest during her remaining days. She found simple things that helped provide order and some sense of control as the days of unknowing turned into weeks and then months of fragile promises for more good days ahead. Through the use of actual e-mail exchanges, Linda's voice, her mother's and siblings' voices, as well as those of friends and caregivers, rise from the pages of this beautiful reflection.

When All That's Left of Me Is Love is a story about learning to let go gracefully while staying in touch completely. Readers will be inspired by a heartbroken family's determination to help a loved one live in the midst of dying. While the book is a detailed portrayal of the author's personal experiences with death, it is also a universal story. I plan to include it in my course on "Love through the Seasons of Death."

This book is truly a testament of love, as the title suggests. It is about love refined and deepened by grief and gratitude. It is a tribute to a mother who loved with her last breath and beyond. It is the story of a daughter who gives herself away through the gift of her pen.

—Sharon G. Thornton, Ph.D.,
Professor of Pastoral Theology
at Andover Newton Theological School

**PALM BEACH COUNTY
LIBRARY SYSTEM
3650 Summit Boulevard
West Palm Beach, FL 33406-4198**

When All That's Left of Me Is Love will take you on a journey into the heart and soul of healing care. It is personal and profound with a simple language a grieving heart can embrace during the most difficult time of life. It is a book that should be on the shelves of anyone facing loss.

—Rev. Sam Oliver, author of *Angel of Promise*
and contributing writer for *Healing Ministry Journal*,
The Journal of Terminal Oncology, and
The American Journal of Hospice and Palliative Care

This book is a wonderful account of the final year and one day of the author's mother's life. The chapters entitled 'Calendars' and 'Happy Hour' are brilliant. I noted several places in the manuscript that I found especially beneficial to readers, including p. 75, the paragraph beginning, 'Each time Mom did something adventurous...' At the top of page 116, I simply wrote, 'I cried.' Linda Campanella offers hope and comfort to those facing a terminal illness by providing a sense of presence and purpose during her mother's illness.

—Matthew Binkewicz, author of *Peaceful Journey:*
A Hospice Chaplain's Guide to End-of-Life

When all
that's left of me
is love

When all that's left of me is love

A Daughter's Story of Letting Go

Linda Campanella

Tate Publishing & Enterprises

When All That's Left of Me Is Love
Copyright © 2011 by Linda Campanella. All rights reserved.

No part of this publication may be reproduced, stored in a retrieval system or transmitted in any way by any means, electronic, mechanical, photocopy, recording or otherwise without the prior permission of the author except as provided by USA copyright law.

The opinions expressed by the author are not necessarily those of Tate Publishing, LLC.

Published by Tate Publishing & Enterprises, LLC
127 E. Trade Center Terrace | Mustang, Oklahoma 73064 USA
1.888.361.9473 | www.tatepublishing.com

Tate Publishing is committed to excellence in the publishing industry. The company reflects the philosophy established by the founders, based on Psalm 68:11,
"The Lord gave the word and great was the company of those who published it."

Book design copyright © 2011 by Tate Publishing, LLC. All rights reserved.
Cover design by Kenna Davis
Interior design by Nathan Harmony

Published in the United States of America

ISBN: 978-1-61777-417-1
1. Family & Relationships / Parenting / Parent & Adult Child
2. Self-Help / Death, Grief, Bereavement
11.07.18

DEDICATION

For my father, in tribute to my mother,
and with gratitude to my husband.

ACKNOWLEDGMENTS

Heartfelt thanks to those beyond my immediate family who read a grieving, grateful daughter's manuscript, offered encouraging feedback and good advice, and ultimately persuaded me to believe I had written something worth sharing more broadly: Julie Bazenas, Kathleen Graham, Stephanie Gunning, Bobye List, Gary Miller, and Faith Sullivan.

Table of contents

Introduction: No Regrets   15

Loving   23

News   25

Epiphany   29

It Goes without Saying, But...   33

Calm, Cool, and Collected...and So Lucky   43

Hope   49

Connecting   57

Quesadillas   61

Living   71

Calendars   73

Good Days, in Ways Big and Small   79

Happy Hour   93

Voodoo Medicine   99

Day Bed   111

Doing   121

Believing   **133**

   The Miracle   135

   The Gift of Giving   141

   A Beginning, Not an End   147

   Medicine for the Heart and Soul   157

Letting Go   **163**

   No More Tears   165

   Holding on while Letting Go   171

   The Birds   183

   Poetry   189

   Love, Always Love   203

   October Twenty-fourth   211

   Final Thoughts   215

Post Script   **223**

KADDISH

Mother of my birth, for how long were we together
    in your love and my adoration of your self?
For the shadow of a moment as I breathed your pain
    and you breathed my suffering, as we knew
of shadows in lit rooms that would swallow the light.

    Your face beneath the oxygen tent was alive
but your eyes were closed. Your breathing was hoarse
but your sleep was with death. I was alone with you
    as it was when I was young but only alone now
    and now with you. I was to be alone forever
    as I was learning, watching you become alone.

Earth is your mother as you were mine, my earth,
    my sustenance, my comfort, and my strength
    and now without you I turn to your mother
    and seek from her that I may meet you again
      in rock and stone: whisper to the stone,
    I love you; whisper to the rock, I found you;
whisper to earth, Mother, I have found my mother
    and I am safe and always have been.
                —David Ignatow

Introduction

NO REGRETS

A few weeks after my mother died, I found I could summon enough courage and strength to pore through my e-mail files looking for messages she had sent me in the past. Reading her words on paper was as close as I could come to hearing her voice again, and I needed to feel that close.

I am one of those folks who delete way too little and save too much, which means my search was relatively fruitful. Even with the abundance, however, I sadly remembered certain things I wish I had not deleted. Among the saved e-mails was one my mother sent me on January 8, 2003, in response to one from me. I no longer have a copy of my e-mail to her, but ostensibly it was a love letter, written in an especially reflective moment following church one Sunday when I learned that my friend Polly's mother had died.

——-Original Message——-
From: Nan & Eck
Sent: Wednesday, January 08, 2003 1:30 PM
To: Linda Campanella
Subject: your very special note written after church

Dear Linda,

This was certainly a lovely note … and, no surprise to you, I'm sure … had me bawling. It arrived just a while ago and, believe it or not, I was looking at an old photo album, specifically to look at old photos of Gram and Gramp. Gramp's death I can deal with … I deal with memories and generally smile. With Gram it's different … and they say, it's never easy to lose a mother. I think of her and of all the things I'd like to tell her and the things I'd like to ask her. *Na ja, so ist es halt.* And my sympathy is with your friend Polly.

It's a bit difficult for anyone, I think, to put thoughts into words when these concern love, gratitude, caring. Thanks for doing so. In return, I'd like to tell you what I hope you know: I love you terribly, too! And it means so much to me that you and your family are nearby … this alone, there's no denying it, makes for a special bond. And I'm very, very grateful to you, Linda. You should *not, not at all* feel "regret—that I never fully felt or acknowledged the void, the pain, you felt and still feel over the loss of your own parents." (Perhaps this sentiment is sort of "a given," however. I feel strong regret … perhaps unfounded in this instance as well, that I didn't give Gram the understanding and support she deserved and surely needed at the time of Nanna's death, and beyond.)

No regrets, Linda … you have ALWAYS been there for me, and best of all is the conviction that you always WILL be there for me (not necessarily as a physical presence) whenever I need you. Please know that I want to be there for you, too, for as long as I live … a mother is a mother forever! (You'll find out!)

Heaps of love (and the following verse I once gave to Gram!), Mom

A Mother and Daughter

Nurtured by time through the highs and the lows,
The love which is theirs ever deepens and grows.
And both turn more patient as days become years,
Growing older and wiser through gladness and tears.

They cling to each other in times of despair,
Taking comfort in knowing the other one's there.
Providing support with a look or a touch,
It's the littlest things, that to them, mean so much!

Deeply concerned for the ones they hold dear,
They mark birthdays and holidays all through the year.
Building family traditions each step of the way,
Sharing good news and bad, as they go day to day.

They're a mother and daughter, and right from the start,
They were forever joined in a place in the heart.
And the lifetime of love which they willingly give,
Will enhance and sustain them as long as they live.
—(author unknown)

In rereading Mom's e-mail, I not only heard her voice, I also felt enveloped in her love and was reminded powerfully, through her words, of the sheer strength of our bond. We were, as the poem she shared suggests, "forever joined in a place in the heart." "Forever" has more meaning to me now that she is gone, and I do find comfort knowing she is still in that special place in my heart where we remain connected. In hindsight, I am particularly thankful I took the time to tell my mother on that occasion in 2003 just how much she meant to me.

The writing of Mom's obituary almost six years later was another occasion to tell her, in no uncertain terms, how much I loved her. Within ten days of her diagnosis in September 2008, she and my father, who together launched immediately into get-her-affairs-in-order mode, shared an "updated" draft of an already-written obituary with their four children, "in case it is needed," as my father put it. Knowing that it was going to be needed long before anyone in the family had ever imagined, I was already in a highly emotional state when I read the draft; I was anticipating the day—sooner, not later—when this extraordinary, loving person would no longer be in the center of my life. In the face of such an overwhelming prospect, the short draft of Mom's obituary, providing key facts of her life, was underwhelming to say the least; this reflected, I suppose, my parents' humility. In its understatement, the obituary was, to me, utterly unacceptable. It provided no sense of who this woman was or any hint that the world was a much, much better place—a *wonderful* place—with her in it. The draft did not suggest how broken our hearts would be or how terribly we would miss her.

From: Linda Campanella
Sent: Friday, September 19, 2008 11:59 AM
To: Eric Sachsse; Claudia S. Barr; Paula Blaker
Subject: RE: NLS etc.

Paula, Claudia, and Eric,
Attached is a readable version of the obituary draft Mom and Dad sent yesterday. Below is the response I sent them immediately.

> *I hope you will allow me to further update (and embellish) the obituary. Whether you allow it or not, I intend to do so—for your review and approval, of course. You have provided the bones; there is some flesh to add (and heart).*
> *XOXOX*
> *LSC*

Between 3:00 and 4:45 a.m., I lay in bed composing. I could not sleep, but I also couldn't bring myself to get out of bed to write down the thoughts that were spinning through my head (and that I was afraid I might forget) regarding the "flesh" and "heart" I wanted to add to her obituary. This morning, thankfully, I remembered many of my earlier thoughts, and I have since composed a draft that I offer now for your review and reaction. It may be hard to read, but I believe it will be easier to read now, while we still hope for and believe in the possibility of many more months and even years with Mom; if her death truly were imminent, an obituary would arguably seem more "real." We can review it now as something we will need some time off in the future.

I want (not that anyone asked me or cares!) very much for her obituary to be a tribute to the person she is and has been. As she has requested no memorial service and no speaking about her at the calling hours/celebration of life, we should celebrate her publicly with an obituary that goes well beyond the draft she and Dad have prepared. I hope you'll agree. Please let me know what you think about my proposed alternative. No hurry. Truly! I am not sharing it with them at this point. Await your feedback/input first.

XOXO

Poo

I didn't have the nerve to show Mom the rewritten obituary, which my siblings supported wholeheartedly, or should I say brokenheartedly, until late November. This was a time when Mom was not feeling well and believed she would not live much longer, and she was making clear to us that she would feel unsettled and thus somewhat unnerved until certain "to-dos" relating to her death had been settled and taken care of. The obituary, as well as planning for the celebration of life following her death, needed to be "checked off the list," so I could not avoid what I knew was going to be a very emotional event any longer. I needed to share my draft with her for her review and blessing, because keeping it from her was causing her some anxiety.

My hesitation to share it with Mom stemmed in part from my not wanting to be weak or sad in front of her, despite my minister's having assured me it was important for someone in her situation to see us cry, to know and to appreciate that her life means so much to us that we could not imagine being happy without her. I could understand this. Nevertheless, knowing how important it was to *her* that she remain strong (for my father), I didn't want my weakness to in turn make her weak. It is hard to explain. Fundamentally, I just wanted her to be happy, not sad, in her final days, weeks, months.

My hesitation also reflected my belief that finalizing an obituary was tantamount to accepting the reality of what an obituary reports. While I had accepted the inevitability of my mother's death, I had gone out of my way in the weeks since her diagnosis to help her focus on living, not dying, and I had tried not to believe or suggest, through words or actions, that death was going to happen as soon as she and my father seemed to think. In the days after her diagnosis, my father had sent an e-mail to his nephews in Germany, which he closed by saying, *auf Deutsch*, "We are hoping for a couple good months." By the end of November, it already had been a couple months.

I shared my draft of her obituary with Mom on one of the days that Dad was working. I had managed to persuade him that it would be good for his emotional well-being and probably also for Mom's if he could continue working two or three days a week at the hospital; I adjusted my own life and priorities so as to become Mom's companion on those days. Late one afternoon, I gave her my draft, explaining that I hoped she would find it acceptable because it was important to me and, indeed, to all her children that people know how deeply she was loved. In those moments together, the tears I had held back in her presence for almost three months flowed freely. I told her how much I loved her and how desperately I didn't want to lose her. In those moments, she shed some of the only tears I saw during what would be a yearlong battle with cancer. I'm not sure I ever felt closer to her—except, perhaps, as death finally approached.

My mother died peacefully at home after an inspiringly courageous fight to live. She *did* live—one year and one day from her diagnosis. The long goodbye was excruciatingly difficult, but in some ways, our family is so grateful for the year we had; it brought us together in extraordinary ways, and we filled the year with much fun and love. Only in the days following her death did I begin to realize just how courageous and strong she was. She never despaired, was not depressed, shed nary a tear, woke up each morning happy to be with us, and went to bed each night feeling thankful. She did far more living than dying, that's for sure.

Nancy L. Sachsse was an incredible woman, as I hope and believe her obituary attests. After her death, many people spoke or wrote to my father specifically about the obituary, sharing thoughts that I know touched him deeply and made him glad we had not published the original and skeletal version of the death announcement. An especially endearing part of her life story was their love story, and this did not go unnoticed.

> *Eckart, such a beautiful write up…just reading it, one could feel the love she had for her family and all of you for her. How lucky for both of you to have shared such a special relationship all those years.*

As incredible as she was, I am not writing this book to tell my mother's story. I could not do justice to it. For now, I will let the obituary speak for itself. I poured my heart into it and cannot do any better. Rather, this book is about the road we traveled together. It is about how she *lived* in her last year (right up to her last week), not about how she died. It is about how she and our family managed to enjoy what was described at the celebration of life as "a magical year." It is about being able to say, "I have no regrets." It is about holding on while letting go.

In recalling the past year and wishing, for reasons I'm still not entirely clear about, to share certain highlights of it, I am able to draw on what amounts to a chronology serendipitously established as a result of my being, in addition to a chronic keeper of e-mails, also a prolific producer of them. I am not particularly proud of either habit and actually have been engaged in an ongoing battle with myself, the goal of which is to e-mail less and talk more, particularly when it comes to professional interactions. There are many reasons why I reflexively pull out the keyboard to write (as opposed to picking up the phone to gab). One primary reason, and it certainly applies in the context of my mother's illness, is that I process my thoughts and emotions by writing. There is something therapeutic and cathartic about the act of putting things down on paper. This act is, for me at least, helpful, calming, focusing, and healing.

So in grieving the loss of my mother (less than two months ago), I have pulled out the keyboard and am writing. Though some of what I am recalling and writing is painful, overall this process surely will help heal the rip in my heart.

I miss my mother more than I can say and every bit as much as I imagined I would, or more. Selfishly, I do hope a little bit of her can live on through what I share on these pages. And if our experience during our last year together can reassure or inspire others who are facing the end of a cherished relationship, then even in death, her generous spirit and big heart will be at work in the world.

Loving

News

Our youngest son went off to college at the end of August 2008, rendering me an "empty-nester." I had mixed emotions about attaining this status. On the one hand, the change was liberating and exciting, to be sure. Having raised three sons—none of them a hellion, but none of them an angel, either—Joe and I were looking forward to the freedom of being able to sneak away to our cabin in the Berkshires or *rendezvous* somewhere with empty-nester friends without worrying about what might be going on back at the homestead in our absence. Actually, there was much to look forward to as we contemplated our existence without any kids in the house on a daily basis.

On the other hand, empty-nester status meant a chapter in my life and also a cherished role that largely defined me were coming to a close. I loved my children and I loved being a mother—*their* mother. A year or so earlier, I had announced to my own mother, with whom I shared virtually everything, that I was coming upon what probably would be a difficult, perhaps traumatic, year: turning fifty, of course menopause, my "baby" going off to college, and the expected death of the family dog, a black Lab named Pepper, who was thirteen at the time and who, since that day of gloomy prognosticating, has continued to defy the odds. At my feet snoring as I write this (on November 9, 2009), she is marching—almost blind, practically deaf, and with hind legs that barely support her anymore—toward her fifteenth birthday! Thank goodness, for if I had lost Pepper, given how the year unfolded, I'm not sure how our family would have coped.

Little over a week after Phil left for Bates, on September 8 at around 5:00 p.m., to be more exact, I received a phone call from my father that began with the dreaded words "Are you sitting down?" Those words belonged in books, movies, and *other* people's lives; what were they suddenly doing in mine? As it turned out, I was rather relieved to be sitting down for the conversation that followed, because the words my father spoke shook the earth beneath me. I remember finding it difficult to breathe. Receiving the news he relayed felt like getting a knee to the gut; the wind was knocked out of me. I don't remember what I said or if I was even able to speak.

I do remember that Dad said, "Here she is," and turned the conversation on his end over to my mother after he had delivered the news. Her calm, matter-of-fact, disarmingly upbeat demeanor in that moment became her trademark.

On several occasions during the months that followed, my mother would say, with a mix of seriousness and levity, that I certainly was getting more than I had bargained for or counted on in this year of anticipated and predicted transitions. "You never thought you'd also lose your mother, did you?" Well, *no!* I did not. Not in my wildest dreams—or, I should say, my worst nightmares. On September 8, 2008, the nightmare and a long good-bye began.

The call from my father delivered the news that my seventy-three-year-old mother and best friend, Nancy, had stage-four small-cell lung cancer with metastases to the brain. There were no symptoms associated with the large mass in her lung that had been found on X-ray when the doctors went looking for a primary tumor. Symptoms attributable to the brain cancer—four secondary tumors visible on an MRI ordered when physical examinations had ruled out ocular reasons for Mom's headache and vision problems—are what had led ultimately to her diagnosis.

It was a diagnosis that stunned not only her family, but also her new primary care physician, who had been methodically seeking explanations for a strange combination of ailments that had been bothering my mother in recent months, none of which led anyone to suspect metastatic lung cancer or a diagnosis modified by the adjectives "incurable" and "terminal." Getting this deadly diagnosis was like drawing the "Go directly to jail" card in *Monopoly*. What bad luck! The trip around the board just got suddenly shorter and a lot less fun. Can't I roll again?

Managing to keep his composure on the phone, my father concluded our conversation by saying, "Your mother is a sick cookie."

My mother? Mom? How could this be? Did I really hear what I think he just told me?

When we hung up, I couldn't move, couldn't breathe, couldn't think. I couldn't even cry. Shock paralyzes. When my senses reawakened, what had seemed numbingly surreal felt frighteningly real, and at that moment, my limp body broke into a sweat and my brain remembered how to let me cry.

Oh my God! Now what? What should I do?

Epiphany

From: Linda Campanella
Sent: Wednesday, September 10, 2008 9:44 AM
To: Claudia Barr; Paula Blaker; Eric Sachsse
Subject: thoughts on living and dying

Tears. More tears. So many tears. No words. Only tears.
What a mess! And how unhelpful! I am writing this to you,
my siblings, but in reality, I am writing it to myself in an effort to process the thoughts that have been in my head and to
talk myself into believing that I know what I should be doing
in the face of news that has shaken my world and broken my
heart. I hope you won't mind my sharing it. This is, for better or worse, one of the ways I am coping. I do not mean to
impose on you or make you any sadder than you are already.
Perhaps what I'm writing in an effort to help myself will in
some small way be helpful to you. I hope so. XOX

In reacting to the news of Mom's cancer, I have been focusing in a reflexive way on what it means in the end: her
death, Dad's being a widower, our losing our mother, memories that will never be because she won't be here, things that
she has perhaps already done or experienced for the last
time. Consequently, the past forty-eight hours have been a
wrenching time of grieving for me. My mind has wandered

to the end, skipping the all-important middle, which is living. During another restless and essentially sleepless night, it struck me suddenly (and thankfully) that I need, for my sake and especially Mom's, to change my perspective. I need to be thinking about life, not death. We have not lost her. She is with us and, God willing, she will be with us for longer than any of us is imagining and fearing right now.

A diagnosis of terminal cancer is perhaps especially terrible in that the end of life, which every one of us faces as an inevitable, is suddenly predictable, within sight. It's a known rather than unknown. There is a timeframe. We know the end is coming sooner than we thought or hoped. When we don't know when we are going to die, we live each day freely and fully, without considering the possibility that this day actually could be our last if a terrible accident happened, or that we might have a fatal heart attack next week, or... Conceivably, Mom could outlive Dad, if you stop to think of it, or even one of us. Possible, but not likely.

Unfortunately, the sense of boundary-less living has been taken from Mom. But she is still living. And there could be joy in every remaining day if she and we carry on, as best we can, without thinking about the fact that we know the end is coming. I do not mean to suggest this will be easy. But I got out of bed this morning feeling as though I could possibly function today if I stopped my premature grieving. She is alive, and she does not want any of us, herself included, to be "glum," as she put it. She's got more living to do before she dies. Yesterday I told Joe I could not imagine how I would be able to carry on in a manner that even remotely felt like "as normal," but I realize this morning that I must. And I must do so in a way that feels and is authentic, not forced or fake. That means being fully in the moment.

She needs to embrace life and we need to, for her and with her, for Dad and with Dad. We need to grill on their deck and celebrate that Autumn Fields is such a great place for them to be. We need to play Hearts. We need to recommend a good book. We need to share happy news of our children with her, and we need to consult her when we face challenges and need her shoulder. We need to make plans—not long-term plans but plans that look beyond today and tomorrow. We need to do ordinary things, because they are the things we would ordinarily do with her in our lives. We need to try, try, try to help her live, before we inevitably will find ourselves helping her die.

I believe her greatest fear is not that she is going to die but that Dad, her love and her hero, is going to have to experience her dying and then somehow try to find the strength to live without her. Arguably, the diagnosis of terminal cancer is harder for those who will survive than on the one who will die—except, perhaps, in the case of someone who, like Mom, is always thinking about and worrying about others. Dad is struggling mightily, and I know we will all collapse emotionally the first, and every, time we see him cry. Mom has already seen it and is, I believe, being strong in the face of her devastating diagnosis for him, for his sake, so that he can be hopeful and stay strong. I realize this morning that I need to be strong for her so that she can be strong for him, even though I might believe she needs to let herself cry. She doesn't want to, she has said. And she did not want me to cry yesterday. I felt I needed to cry with her before I could go on with the normal chit-chatty conversations she is wanting and trying to have. What I need doesn't matter.

If she wants chit-chat, I will deliver. She wants to live! She said that she fears losing her sense of humor. We need to make sure she has plenty to smile at and laugh about. The cloud will always be hovering overhead in the days, weeks, and (hopefully) many months ahead, but there can still be plenty of sunshine on cloudy days.

For partly selfish reasons, I am relieved that this epiphany, or whatever it was, hit me in the middle of the night. I do not want to imagine life without her, for me and especially for Dad. It is too painful, and I am too sad when my mind wanders there. I have been completely undone by grief these past forty-eight hours, so I will focus on the living still to do, not on the dying that we now know is coming much sooner than we ever imagined.

I will concentrate on and believe in the possibility that treatments are going to be very effective in helping her feel good and extending her life so that there will be many happy memories to come in the months and maybe even years to come.

I will believe in the power of positive thinking and will invest my energy in willing her to live long and helping her, and Dad, live life as close to "normal" as possible.

I will help the sun break through on cloudy days.

It goes without saying, but...

From: Linda Campanella
Sent: Monday, September 15, 2008 3:23 PM
To: Nan & Eck
Subject:

Mom,

It goes without saying, but it shouldn't go unsaid, even though (and I regret this) it might make you sad to hear/read it: My heart is breaking.

I am strong, I am being strong, and I *will* be strong; but I'm not superhuman. I have cried buckets. I'm not the only one.

There. I said it. Please don't be sad. I just want to be 100 percent sure you know it. You're a heartbreaker! And what a wonderful commentary on one's life that is. I suppose it's something to be wished for. You are so deeply loved, and when the day comes (a long time from now, we hope) that you are no longer with us physically, your presence and your love will be missed terribly. Certainly by me.

You are the best mother (and grandmother and mother-in-law, as well) anyone could ever want. And I have always wanted you (and Dad) to live forever!

It will be good to get past this current diagnostic/prognostic stage of things, with death and dying so much on our minds and hearts, so that we can concentrate on life and get on with all the living—the joyful living—still to be done!

Speaking of which … Are you coming to visit tomorrow? ☺

XOX

Poo

My three siblings and I all, but each independently, felt it necessary to send my mother an "it goes without saying, but it should not go unsaid" message. Mine you read above; and my brother's you'll see below, along with Mom's loving response. I had a copy of this exchange between the two of them because Mom had "secretly" shared it with me (a secret I let Eric in on). Following our mother's diagnosis, the four of us tried not to succumb to feelings of sadness, and on the surface we managed to do pretty well. Soon, though, I think we worried just a bit that, as a result of our being/acting strong and hopeful and optimistic, Mom might somehow miss the fact that we were all indescribably shaken and sad.

Each of us had expected and wanted her to live to be an old lady. None of us wanted her to have to go through the angst and everything else that comes with a battle against cancer. All of us loved her from the very bottoms of our hearts. She was not perfect (Who is?), but she was the best mother any of us could imagine having.

From: Nan & Eck
Sent: Friday, September 26, 2008 9:53 AM
To: Linda Campanella
Subject: Fw: Running Commentary

Maybe I shouldn't, but forwarding (secretly) to you anyway … sharing seems to be what I want most. XOXO

———- Original Message———-
From: Nan & Eck
To: Eric Sachsse
Sent: Friday, September 26, 2008 6:48 AM
Subject: Re: Running Commentary

Oh, my sweet son. I don't cry, but words like these bring me close! Eric, I know you well. I know everything that is in your heart about me, just as you surely know, without words, all that rests in my heart about you. We have always been a great mother-son combo. Nanna called you her champion. I loved that and took over the phrase! Be well, Eric, and be happy in a long and wonderful life ahead. I have such faith that this will be the case. Always, Mom

Dear Mom,

I'm sitting here taking a break from organizing my thoughts and planning my day and days ahead and started thinking about you, as I often do. And it occurred to me that maybe it doesn't go without saying ... so I'll say it: I am so, so sorry you are sick with cancer. I don't know how to fully process (and clearly haven't yet done so) what your illness means in terms of the future. Too weird and surreal, isn't it? And obviously so very sad and upsetting, but I don't focus on that ... and I know you don't want me/us to.

Anyway, even though I perhaps haven't said it (enough), I do think about you every day throughout each day. And I love you very much. And I am very proud of how you are approaching and handling everything, and that won't change even if/when the situation temporarily gets the better of you ... which I have no doubt it will (and perhaps already has).

You are special and so very much loved.

Always your son and always with love, Eric

A few weeks after Mom died, I received in the mail a *CareNotes* pamphlet entitled "Losing Your Mom." It was written by Peggy

Heinzmann Ekerdt and had been sent to me by a volunteer at my church. Several things in that little booklet seemed to say what I had been thinking or feeling or fearing:

When a mother dies, the loss of unconditional love is often a loss that no one else can understand, much less fill.

When a mother dies, we lose a piece of who we are. We lose the person whose story provides the beginning of our own, whose sense of self greatly impacts who we are. It is not unusual to wonder: If I am no longer my mother's child, then who am I?

When a mother dies, we lose the person who rejoices in our accomplishments and agonizes in our struggles; the person who thinks we should win every race, woo every beau or belle, and succeed at every job; the person whose first urge is to protect, shelter, and guide us; the person who knows what is best for us, or thinks she does; the person who brags about us in our absence and offers expert advice in our presence. In sum, we lose the person who is our biggest fan and our most ardent defender.

Clearly, the author must have known our mother! What she wrote—especially that last paragraph—is all about the mother whose loss my siblings and I had already begun to mourn. Judy Ball, in another *CareNotes* pamphlet, this one entitled "Grieving the Loss of Your Parent," wrote, "We may have lived through years to be an adult, but we will always be a child in relation to our parents. Even if we find ourselves 'parenting our parents' before their deaths, it is the parent of our youth and childhood that we bury." Eric, Claudia, Paula, and I were not ready to bury the parent of our youth and childhood ... and of our adulthood.

Each of us reacted to the news differently, coped differently, expressed love differently, "parented our parent" differently, and eventually grieved differently. There was an occasional moment of tension, but when these moments arose, they could be and were attributed, on the one hand, to our unique natures (despite common gene pools) and, on the other hand, to the emotionally stressful and often physically draining circumstances in which we found our-

Linda Campanella

selves. There was never any question that, even when we did or saw things differently, we all were motivated by the same boundless love we felt for both our parents (whom our children, and sometimes we ourselves, call Nan and Opa).

I lived closest to Enfield, just a half hour away in West Hartford. Eric lived two hours away in New Hampshire. Claudia was three and a half hours away (or, too often, six with traffic!) in New Jersey. Paula was in Ferndale, Washington, which, after Mom's diagnosis, felt like a world away. Geographically we were dispersed, but we tried to stay close in spirit. E-mail and cell phones helped connect us.

From: Eric Sachsse
Sent: Wednesday, September 10, 2008 10:35 AM
To: Linda Campanella; Claudia Barr; Paula Blaker
Subject: RE: thoughts on living and dying

I have not called you guys because I really don't want to talk about it … Any phone call would be about ten seconds long with me not knowing what to say. I just don't have anything (or much of anything) to say about it other than it sucks and I'm in some weird form of mild shock about it. I sobbed in short bursts a few times on my porch Monday night after I had called them and got the unexpected and unwelcome news. I've welled up a couple/few times since when I thought sentimental thoughts and when I told Eva and B last evening. But I have not cried buckets as it sounds like Linda has. Maybe I'm not fully facing it, I don't know. People react differently … plus, it just doesn't seem real. I guess I cannot quite comprehend it emotionally, even though I get it mentally. There, I guess I did have something to say about all this, just not over the phone.

I enjoyed a couple of fun, light-hearted conversations with Nan and Opa yesterday, B had a nice chat with them last night too, and Nan and I had a very early and upbeat e-mail exchange this morning, so Linda will be glad to know that I am certainly on board with the "enjoy the moment and help Nan live life" aspect of this.

Hope you're all more or less well. I am.

From: Paula Blaker
Sent: Wednesday, September 10, 2008 1:00 PM
To: Linda Campanella; Claudia S. Barr; Eric Sachsse
Subject: RE: thoughts on living and dying

I feel very far away, much farther than I felt while in Laos. It is a difficult time for all of us, especially Nan and Opa, and there is no way to know how this will play out and how we are supposed to play the game.

I agree we should lean on each other for support so, as Linda said, we can be strong for them.

Right now, I am not feeling strong.

Much love to you all,

Paula

From: Linda Campanella
Sent: Monday, September 15, 2008 8:56 AM
To: Claudia S. Barr; Paula Blaker; Eric Sachsse
Subject: today

I am thinking of all of you as we sit, together but miles apart, on pins and needles awaiting the latest news to be delivered later today following further tests. No matter what it is, I'm afraid we will continue to occupy the space that exists between disbelief and grief in the days and weeks ahead. But right now, in this moment... I am very hopeful.

XOXO

From: Claudia Barr
Sent: Monday, September 15, 2008 9:40 AM
To: Linda Campanella; Paula Blaker; Eric Sachsse
Subject: RE: today

Very nice. There's comfort in knowing I'm not the only one on pins and needles. It's true, we're miles apart ... but together.

Hugs to each of you,

Claudia

Each of us played a slightly different role during the course of the year, and I believe all of us appreciated each other for what we did to try to support our parents. We also supported each other. I am thankful for all three of my siblings, thankful not to have been an only child.

My proximity to Enfield, and my being an empty-nester who also was her own boss in a private consulting practice and thus more or less able to control workload, made it logical and possible for me to be very present in my parents' lives during the year following diagnosis. With total support and understanding from my husband, Joe, I was in Enfield *a lot* ... many days every week ... for twelve months.

If I did any good during the early months especially, it was as a diversion from what surely must have been, for both Mom and Dad, a preoccupation with the diagnosis and prognosis. For the few hours here and there when I was with them, we were just being, doing, living. She was healthy enough that "normal" could prevail during such interactions.

On so many nights, I drove home in tears or held back the tears until I got home and Joe saw the sadness in my eyes. He would signal to me with his eyes that it would be okay to cry, and so I did. I remember vividly the many occasions when I would say good-bye to my folks in a very upbeat tone, hold myself together long enough to pull out of the driveway, and then be hit by what I can only describe as a "wall of grief." It felt like a physical assault to the gut that released uncontrollable and loud sobs. I suppose I was wailing. Occasionally, I could hold myself together long enough to call one of my siblings with an update. They always were curious for a firsthand account of how both parents were coping. I couldn't get through those conversations without releasing my grief either.

> From: Linda Campanella
> Sent: Tuesday, September 16, 2008 8:55 PM
> To: Claudia Barr; Eric Sachsse; Paula Blaker
> Subject: FW: we're home

I brought two wig options to Enfield tonight, and we've got a winner. I think Mom is really quite pleased and relieved. Dad didn't even know she had it on; we actually had a little "fun" (if you can believe it) during the "dress-up"/try-on session. We'll *rendezvous* in West Hartford next week for a consultation/fitting with the expert to make sure size is right.

By the way, Dr. Hetzel (oncologist for chemo) did call while I was there, and he wants to meet with Mom and Dad two weeks into the three-week radiation therapy (on September 30) to discuss chemo strategy. It seemed to me that Dad was a little relieved (hopeful?) that chemo may be an option. Not for a cure, however; the concern (expectation) is that her lung tumors will grow (and they will) and cause serious problems for her. My hope (and perhaps Dad's secret hope) is that the chemo will do more than thwart growth. A period of remission would be wonderful.

They are doing well. I find it comforting to see them functioning at all, which is why I'm telling you. I think my visits are good in that they distract from what surely is preoccupying them. I work hard at it in a way that feels natural and authentic. Really. All in all, they do seem to be doing okay. Tonight we grilled. I played rummy with Dad. He planted a couple mums. The three of us played some Hearts after dinner. We tuned into the Red Sox briefly (and looked for Eric!). We talked about Essex, about family, about "stuff." A nice call from Claudia came, and Mom clearly enjoyed chatting. They are (and she especially is) very strong. I manage to keep myself together and then a tidal wave of something (sadness, grief…) hits me as soon as I leave, and I cry with moans (an explosion) because I've been holding in my emotions for so long. They do want us to be strong. It helps them. It especially helps Mom, who is, as she wrote last night, 100 percent committed to staying strong for Dad.

LSC

My sisters and brother were grateful to me for the time I was spending in Enfield, and at the same time, they were, I know, envious. Especially in the early weeks and months, when we had no clue as to the course Mom's disease would take, we had the ominous feeling that days were numbered, rendering every opportunity to be with Mom a gift. As the closest one, I was the one receiving this gift in relative abundance. While my siblings were envious of that, they also anticipated, again with appreciation, that I would pay a relatively heavy toll—emotionally, physically, and in many unforeseen ways—as a primary caregiver.

From: Linda Campanella
Sent: Tuesday, September 16, 2008 9:16 PM
To: Claudia Barr; Eric Sachsse; Paula Blaker
Subject: RE: We're home

It was good to cry with/to you on my drive home, Claudia. Thanks.

By the way, I do not want or deserve your thanks. I wrote the following to Paula this morning in response to something she had said or written, and it's probably wise to share it with you and Eric as well. I'm just doing what I can and what I am sure you all would do if you were in my shoes.

I am so relieved that one of us is nearby. I don't see it as a burden, though I know I will experience pain and despair that thankfully those who are not so close geographically may be spared. The Spirit (call it God or whatever you might believe) works in strange, sometimes wonderful ways. I am no longer a slave to the corporate world. My children have just left home. My workload, which was essentially all-consuming for the first half of this year, is light at the moment. I have time and flexibility that, just a month ago, I didn't enjoy. I am able to be where I need and want to be right now. My priorities are very clear. None of you other "children" need feel the least bit guilty about not being as "on call" and available as I am. It's just the way it is. I understand, though, that mixed with any guilt you might feel (and hopefully quickly dismiss), there is also some envy that I am close enough to have time with Mom, especially since we all now know and are coming to accept that time with her is/will be a precious commodity. Yes, I'll have more moments with her, and for that I am deeply grateful.

XOXO

All of us managed to spend much time in Enfield over the roller-coaster course of a year that, through its ups and downs and twists and turns, produced frights and delights, first times and last times, tears and triumphs, epiphanies and confessions, grief and growth. Ultimately, all of us experienced moments for which we will be eventually, and then forever, grateful. And in the final analysis, all four of us did everything we could to love our mother to death, literally, and to surround our father with the love and support he needed as well.

Calm, cool, and collected... and so lucky

From: Nan & Eck
Sent: Tuesday, September 09, 2008 4:45 AM
To: Linda Campanella
Subject: Re:

Hi, sweetie. Dad and I got some good sleep with the help of sleeping pills until a short time ago. Now I got up to take one of the steroid pills that shoulc reduce swellling and help with headache (and perhaps the vision problems that make it so hard to type!), and I hope Dad can roll overr and fall asleep again. Not sleeping is not good... mainly because the mind then takes over and seeks out things I have to try not to think of... namely Dad and my grandchildren and what I'll never know about them. Oh well. Mind control is going to be a priority; I see that now. And I'll manage it!

From: Nan & Eck
Sent: Tuesday, September 09, 2008 10:13 AM
To: Linda Campanella
Subject: Re:

What would I do in this situation without my sweetheart? I am the luckiest person! *Glueck im Unglueck* , FOR SURE!

From: Nan & Eck
Sent: Tuesday, September 09, 2008 10:42 AM
To: Linda Campanella; Eric Sachsse;
Claudia S. Barr; Paula Blaker
Subject: Hopeful, but

I have to say this…

I *am* being hopeful. Never give up! But it is wise also to be a realist. Chest X-ray a year ago was entirely normal. So the good-sized tumor now showing is probably fast-growing. *You* all have to be realistic also!

Also should say this…

Dad is my superhero. I do not know *what* I would do without him in all this. He is being wonderful in every way, but he is having a hard time of it. (Please delete this e-mail and do not "reply.") I think he is going to need your love and support a good bit more than I. My poor sweetheart!

Thanks for all phone call, e-mails…all the love and support, which we know will continue. XOXO

NLS

From: Nan & Eck
Sent: Saturday, September 13, 2008 8:11 PM
To: Linda Campanella
Subject: Re:

Although I'm tired, today was anything but a bad day. I'm obviously feeling strong (and pigging out on rum raisin…life is too short!) but will be in totally unknown territory once therapy begins. Hoping that will not turn me into a limp wimp, but who knows...I am as prepared as I can be for anything. Smile...and sleep well. What wonderful children...entire family, in-laws, grandkids, everyone...I have! Friends too. *So lucky!*And Dad is my biggest prize. Big hugs, Mom

From: Nan & Eck
Sent: Monday, September 15, 2008 3:39 AM
To: Linda Campanella
Subject: the witchung huor again

I have been up, admiring a little bouquet brought by a neighbor from a shower today and sitting on the deck...eating rum raisin (would be nicer if it were with you and drinking wine!) and *fondling my thick hair!* Silly, isn't it? But it was so nice out there. Lovely breeze, crickets happy and singing their hearts out, even caught sight, in the light shining through LR window, of a couple of deer...who also should be sleeping. Nice life. I've had it so good, such a good ride! Back to bed. XOXO

From: Nan & Eck
Sent: Tuesday, September 16, 2008 2:55 AM
To: Linda Campanella; Claudia S. Barr; Paula Blaker
Subject: tjr witching hour asgin. esrly s.m. 9–16

I am doing just fine, but Dad is not. That is why I am writing (and why you will delete). He sits with me on the deck and says, "Well, sweetie, you're going to die from this. You know that," and then puts his head in his hands and sobs. Well, of course I'm going to die, but so is everybody! I remain calm, cool, and collected. Talk logically, comfortingly, I hope, of the day two kids, twenty-one and twenty-four years old...complete innocents...met and fell in love that day and have been in love since then. Magical. We had no idea what we were doing. Isn't it magic? What a blessed life! What memories! I have a huge responsibility to him, and I know for sure that this is what gives me my strength. I have to be strong, for him, and I will be. I know that now for sure. It is my mission and I will not fail…but he will need so much help. I know you all will always be there for him. He is going to need you all so very badly. I can count on you, on you and on the huge support group he will have (has earned so completely). Everyone will help him. Just promise me you will do whatever you can. I love him so much. I want him to find happiness again some day. Thank God I am in such a good emotional state. I will keep it up. It really is not hard.

I have now eaten too much fruit. What kind of idiot am I? This is so weird! Oh well, this is about all I have to say. Let's just all try to keep Dad sane and physically healthy. He has to eat! He sleeps okay (praises be). My mind is going, right? I hope that doesn't really happen!

Upwards and onwards. Going back to bed. I hate doing all this to you all! What a huge and miserable burden I (we) are placing on you! But at some point, I guess it happens in every family. Be strong yourselves and take care of yourselves! How I wish this didn't have to be! But I repeat, everything will be okay! You all will be fine. And I am not one whit worried about myself. No fears at all. And no regrets! Love you all so much…my children, my adored (yes!) sons-in-law, my best-in-the-world grandchildren. So lucky. So lucky. Always with you in love, Mom

From: Nan & Eck
Sent: Tuesday, September 30, 2008 2:30 AM
To: Linda Campanella; Eric Sachsse; Claudia S. Barr; Paula Blaker
Cc: eckart sachsse
Subject:

Went to bed around 10:30 and slept soundly. Woke around 1:30 needing to pee. Then to the kitchen for a glass of cool water; thrush is very prickly and needs soothing. Then Opa appeared…wanted rum raisin. I joined him in the den with a yogurt. Then he told me I should go back to bed, I needed sleep. I really don't need sleep; it seems such a waste of time. Eternity is a long time.

I have to remind myself that you all have lives and do not wish to spend all your time reading about mine!

Hugs,
NLS

Hope

Within my family, I'm notorious for *Googling*. Think of it as trawling for answers. I have a voracious appetite for information, and that appetite is insatiable when my ignorance gives rise to a feeling of impotence. Information and knowledge make me feel less out of control. Equipped with facts or evidence, I feel I can control a situation rather than be controlled by it. (Within the family I also enjoy a reputation as someone who enjoys being in control!)

Faced with a crisis that gives rise to fear or despair, some people turn to prayer. I turned to the Internet. Feeling utterly undone by the news of my mother's diagnosis, I went immediately to www. google.com ... *stage iv small-cell lung cancer treatment prognosis* ...

My *Google* search was not simply a quest for information. It was a desperate hunt for hope. I understood what "stage IV" meant. As Mom herself put it very clearly to us, "There *is* no stage five, you know." I also understood, of course, the meaning of the word "incurable." Given the disease's progression, whatever treatment she might undergo would be palliative, not curative. Got it. However, I did *not* know the answer to the all-important question one naturally contemplates (even if one does not have the courage to ask it outright) when there is a diagnosis of terminal cancer: *How long?*

The honest and entirely unsatisfying answer is that there is no answer to that question, at least no definitive answer. I knew this even before my *Googling* began. But I wanted a range—one with an upper end that counteracted oppressive feelings of gloom and doom. I wanted to be reassured that my mother would live and be in my life for much longer than she and my father seemed to believe initially.

> From: Nan & Eck
> Sent: Monday, September 15, 2008 12:20 PM
> To: Linda Campanella; Eric Sachsse;
> Claudia S. Barr; Paula Blaker
> Subject: update
>
> Hello! Everything under control, albeit a bit overwhelming for both of us.
>   Saw radiation oncologist at 8:30. Start radiation tomorrow. Five days a week (this week just four) for three weeks. Hope to get early appointment Friday morning so I can go to Essex for weekend. Will definitely lose every strand of hair after the first week and will probably not have much energy.
>   Saw medical oncologist 11:00 a.m. No chemo until after radiation. Plan to be worked out after pathology report is out sometime today and then over the next days. No idea what will be decided. You know, of course, there is no cure for me. Essentially, it will become a quality of life issue. Maybe I can get some really good days still ahead! Hope so. Will do my best.
>   That's it in a nutshell…really nothing more to say/write. Everyone being *very* nice. I'm feeling good and thinking good thoughts.
>   Love to you all! XOXOX NLS

I certainly wanted to believe that Mom had more than "some really good days" to look forward to, which is why I did a ton of reading about lung cancer. But I'm not sure any of us really wants a *definitive* answer in the final analysis. Rather than welcoming tomorrow, we might dread it, as each new day would bring us closer to the finish line.

If we know when death will come, it seems to me living would be a process of approaching death on a deadline, not an opportunity for embracing life for as long as it might last. We knew my mother's life was going to be cut short, but we didn't know exactly how short. Medicine is an inexact science, after all (despite society's tendency to ascribe superhuman powers and infallibility to physicians). Moreover, while there is evidence to suggest what the life-extending benefits of radiation and chemotherapy might be, there is no way to calculate the power of positive thinking or the salutary effects of prayer. I believe both these non-medical interventions may have added months to my mother's life. More on that later.

My point for now is that when we don't have a target, we don't know how close to it we are getting. In our case, we tried to welcome each day as an opportunity to do some more living rather than as a day that brought us a step closer to death. Optimism trumped fatalism.

From: Linda Campanella
To: Nan & Eck
Cc: Eric Sachsse; Claudia Barr; Paula Blaker
Sent: Tuesday, September 16, 2008 8:33 PM
Subject: hope

I had a wonderful time tonight. I love you both so much. But that's not the reason for this e-mail. Joe just came up from the poker game in the basement to see how I was doing and how you are doing *and* to tell me that poker buddy Rick knows someone diagnosed with stage IV lung cancer who is alive five years later! I know everyone is different, and I know you may not (and in all likelihood will not) live five years, or even close to it. But please *believe* that it is possible for you to return to Essex next summer, for you to celebrate your fifty-second wedding anniversary, for you to invest in a second and third and tenth or twelfth wig if they only last 3–4 months, for you to be the odds-defying survivor, for who knows what memory is still waiting to be made! Yes, I accept that this friggin' cancer will be the cause of your death. Your death *too soon*. But let's be hoping for and really *believing it possible* to enjoy more than just a couple good, pain-free months. You have great doctors, the best family in the world, and *incredible* strength. Throw healthy doses of hope and faith into the mix with love, strength, and medicine, and who knows how the story will end!

So as you sit on the deck in the dark (eating key lime pie!) in the middle of the night again tonight (unless you are lucky and sleep through), call to mind the inspiring, hope-filled words below. I found them this morning with the intention of forwarding them but then decided not to send them, lest I seem preachy or morose. But now I really, really believe them and want to share them; I am *hopeful*. To have hope we must *believe* that good things are truly possible. I do. I really do. I'm prepared for worse than I'm hoping for, but I *believe* in the possibility of better…

Don't lose hope. When it gets darkest, the stars come out.
—*Unknown.*

In the dark dreary nights, when the storm is at its most fierce, the lighthouse burns bright so the sailors can find their way home again. In life the same light burns. This light is fueled with love, faith, and hope. And through life's most fierce storms these three burn their brightest so we also can find our way home again.
—*Unknown.*

Turn your face to the sun and the shadows fall behind you.
—*Maori Proverb.*

All my love always,
Poo

From: Linda Campanella
To: Nan & Eck
Sent: Wednesday, September 17, 2008 8:58 AM
Subject: more on hope

I probably shouldn't be reading, but I am a glutton for information. (No surprise to you there!) So here I share something I found. I won't do it again, because I know full well that any input from me (other than perhaps a question) regarding medicine is apt to be ill-advised (even if well-intentioned) and totally uninvited. But this is a rather hopeful (though realistic/sobering at the same time) tidbit, *particularly* given how Dad ended his e-mail to Friedl, which I was invited to read, and also in light of Dr. Hetzel's plans to meet with you on September 30. (The bold highlighting is on purpose.)

*Effectiveness of Treatment—Chemotherapy is of **clear benefit** in patients with SCLC. The **likelihood of responding to chemotherapy with or without radiation therapy is quite high**. Response rates of 80 to 100 percent are seen in patients with limited disease, and approximately one-half of these are complete (no remaining evidence of the cancer by either physical examination or X-ray studies). **With extensive stage disease, 60 to 80 percent of patients will respond to chemotherapy, and between 15 and 40 percent will have a complete response**.*

*Despite these favorable results, SCLC tends to recur or relapse within **one to two years** in the majority of patients, particularly those with extensive stage disease. If the SCLC recurs or fails to respond to one type of chemotherapy regimen, a different type of chemotherapy regimen may offer some relief from symptoms and a modest improvement in survival.*

Let's not forget poker buddy Rick's acquaintance, who's doing well five years post-diagnosis with stage IV lung cancer. Or the forty-four-year-old stage IV colon cancer survivor profiled in the *Hartford Courant* last week who's doing great nine years later. Hope…

And all that said, I understand and respect completely your comments regarding the importance of *quality* of life versus length of life. You have my full support on that front, no matter what we confront in the days/weeks/months/years ahead.

Meanwhile, one day at a time … Hope today will be a *good* day. As usual, nice to see the sun shining. It helps one's mood. As does music, so get those CDs spinning!

XOX

LSC

From: Linda Campanella
Sent: Thursday, September 18, 2008 5:40 PM
To: Eric Sachsse
Subject: FW: more on hope

This (see e-mail to Mom and Dad above) is the best I can offer in terms of thoughts about timeframe. I reference an e-mail from Dad to Friedl, in which he wrote that they are hoping for "a couple good months." I truly believe there is reason to have higher hopes, and I believe they may be open to this possibility and maybe even gravitating toward such hope. They are, I believe, encouraged by the prospect of chemo; her type of cancer responds well apparently, although it is sure to recur and will respond less well the second time around if we believe what we read and hear. (One line that I cut out of the blurb above was a line that said, "without chemo the timeframe is a matter of weeks, not months.")

It is still, as it has been from the first moment the reality hit, a question of when, not whether. And Mom has made clear that for her, quality of life is a bigger consideration (goal) than length of life; if chemo is making her utterly miserable, she'll have a choice to make. My hunch is that she won't celebrate her seventy-fifth birthday next October, but I will not stop thinking it well within the realm of possibility that she might.

Meanwhile I keep reinforcing, in whatever way I can without being obnoxious or boring, that we have good reason to be hopeful. I believe you read what I wrote on that subject a couple days ago. All that said, we may have a much clearer sense of timeframe (and perhaps less reason to be hopeful) once the two of them meet with the oncologist for the chemo regimen on September 30.

Linda

P.S. Relative to the blurb above, Mom has "extensive stage," not "limited stage."

LSC

My hunch was right: As it turned out, my mother did *not* live to celebrate her seventy-fifth birthday in October 2009. But she did celebrate a Thanksgiving, Christmas, Valentine's Day, Easter, Mother's Day, Fourth of July, and her fifty-second wedding anniversary on August 17, a feat that seemed implausible if not impossible to her when she was diagnosed in September 2008. With each passing holiday celebration, however, it became easier for her, and us, to imagine and even expect that she would be around for the next one. Why not? And so we pulled out the calendar; we made plans.

If I had found or been given an answer to the question "*How long?*" I would have found it immeasurably more difficult, and arguably even impossible, to live with the hope that buoyed me during the last year of my mother's life. The fact that she died exactly one year and one day from her diagnosis makes me wonder if perhaps she had set a goal when she first contemplated the question herself on one of those sleepless nights when she sat on her deck staring at the stars, eating key lime pie or rum-raisin ice cream, and letting her mind wander as she contemplated her fate. I'd like to think she resolved that, despite the odds of dying much sooner, she would like to live a whole year. *Please, God, let me live for just one more year.*

Connecting

From: Nan & Eck
Sent: Wednesday, September 17, 2008 5:17 AM
To: Linda Campanella
Cc: Eric Sachsse; Claudia Barr; Paula Blaker
Subject: Re: hope

I HAVE FOUND THE TRICK TO MAKE TYPING EASIER… ALL CAPS!

DEARS,

THIS E-MAIL IS IN RESPONSE TO LINDA'S LOVELY ONE BELOW, BUT I WRITE TO ALL OF YOU BECAUSE CONNECTION—NOW ESPE-CIALLY—MAKES ME FEEL SO GOOD. I WRITE FOR ME, I THINK, MORE THAN FOR YOU. YES, I HAVE BEEN SITTING FOR A WHILE ON THE DECK. LOVELY AND COOL, MY KIND OF TEMPS. THE MOON! HAVE YOU SEEN IT? FULL AND GORGEOUS! NO, THIS MIDDLE OF THE NIGHT I HAVE **NOT** BEEN EATING BUT SIPPING SPRITE. I PIGGED OUT ON KEY LIME CHEESECAKE **BE-FORE BED** THIS TIME.

I TOO HAD A WONDERFUL TIME TONIGHT, POO. I CAN'T BELIEVE ALL THE STUFF YOU BROUGHT.

YOU WERE A DEAR TO DO SO MUCH RE-SEARCHING OF WIGS. I KNOW I REBELLED, BUT I AM GLAD YOU DID THIS FOR ME. I WILL DEFI-NITELY GO TO WEST HARTFORD NEXT WEEK AND CONSULT. IT WILL BE GOOD INDEED TO HAVE ONE. I'M NOT A PRETTY BALDIE, AND A WIG WILL PROBABLY WORK AND GIVE ME A BOOST. IF NOTHING ELSE, IT WILL BE FUN TO LAUGH AND JOKE ABOUT, AND THAT'S MY "THING." THANK YOU.

LINDA'S THOUGHTS/QUOTES BELOW ARE LOVELY. I TAKE THEM TO HEART, ALL OF THEM. I HAVE HOPE, A LOT OF IT, FOR SOME REALLY GOOD DAYS AHEAD, HOWEVER MANY THEY MAY BE. THE TIME LINE IS ACTUALLY NOT OF THE **GREATEST** INTEREST. THE QUALITY OF LIFE **IS.** HOW I WOULD LIKE (HOPE?) TO GO OUT WITH A BANG INSTEAD OF A WHIMPER! WHINERS AND COMPLAINERS AND MOANERS ARE HARD TO BE WITH. BUT WHAT WILL BE WILL BE, AND I AM (WE ARE ALL, I GUESS) PRE-PARED FOR ANYTHING. BUT ALL OF YOU WILL HELP ME KEEP MY SPIRITS UP, RIGHT?

FAMILY AND FRIENDS ARE ONE'S GREATEST ASSET. HOW CLEARLY THAT COMES TO FOCUS NOW. **THINGS AND BELONGINGS**...SUCH SIDE-LINE ISSUES...EVEN HEALTH. ONE CAN LIVE A GOOD LIFE EVEN WHEN NOT VERY HEALTHY; LOOK AROUND YOU! BUT CONNECTION IS EV-ERYTHING. CHERISH CONNECTION TO YOUR FAMILY AND FRIENDS MORE THAN ANYTHING ELSE IN THE WORLD FOR THE REST OF YOUR LIVES, MY DEAR ONES. THIS IS PROBABLY THE **ONLY** ADVICE I FEEL LIKE GIVING TO YOU.

RANDOM THOUGHTS (VERY RANDOM):

THE IDEA TO KEEP THE CDS PLAYING EVERY DAY IS AN EXCELLENT ONE. I CAN LOAD FIFTY

AT A TIME ON THE PLAYER, AND I THINK THAT SOON (MAYBE WITH SOMEONE'S HELP) I WILL LOAD FIFTY FAVORITES. I HAVE MANY, MANY DISCS. CLAUDIA, YOU KNOW THAT; I THINK YOU GAVE ME A THOUSAND! IT WILL BE NICE TO HAVE PLEASANT BACKGROUND ALL DAY ... NICE FOR ME AND FOR ANYONE WHO STOPS BY.

I WILL ENJOY ESSEX THIS WEEKEND. I FEEL SURE. THE WEATHER WILL PROBABLY BE NICE!

PEOPLE ARE BEING WONDERFUL TO ME. **PEOPLE ARE INNATELY GOOD.** ISN'T THAT A HAPPY THOUGHT? SURE, THERE ARE BAD APPLES. I DON'T MEET MANY OF THEM, FORTUNATELY. I AM SURROUNDED BY LOVE AND KINDNESS AND GOODNESS. OH, THE E-MAILS, THE THANK YOUS I WANT TO WRITE! I MAY NOT EVER, EVER GET TO THEM ALL! BUT FOLKS WILL UNDERSTAND. YOU ALL CAN SOMEDAY LET FRIENDS KNOW HOW DEEPLY GRATEFUL AND APPRECIATIVE I AM. I EXPECT I MAY PESTER FRIENDS ON THE PHONE IN THE DAYS TO COME. THIS KIND OF CONNECTION IS WHAT WILL KEEP ME AFLOAT AND **CHEERFUL.** MORE THAN ANYTHING, I THINK, I WANT TO BE CHEERFUL. SO FAR I CERTAINLY AM. YOU CAN SEE THAT, CAN'T YOU? AND SO FAR I AM STRONG ... YES, I CERTAINLY AM! I FEEL STRONG AND POSITIVE, AND LIVING FROM JUST ONE DAY TO THE NEXT, I HAVE DISCOVERED, IS A VERY GOOD THING. I HAVE ALSO LEARNED THAT I CAN, WITHOUT GUILT, SIT BACK AND BE DONE FOR. **WOW!** THAT IS SO NOT ME, BUT WHAT A LUXURY ... AND I AM READY TO ALLOW IT! MIND-BOGGLING. GOOD THINGS COME FROM BAD, *JA?*

WHEN I SAT DOWN TO TYPE, I THOUGHT I HAD MANY, MANY RANDOM THOUGHTS. GUESS

NOT SO MANY RIGHT NOW. BE PREPARED, THOUGH, FOR FUTURE RAMBLINGS. I HAVE NO CREATIVE MUSE ANYMORE, BUT I'M AS GABBY AS EVER. YOU MAY FORWARD THIS TO ANYONE YOU CHOOSE. IT IS BLAB, BLAB, BLAB....BUT IT IS ME. CONNECTING. DEAREST LOVE TO YOU ALL, NLS

Quesadillas

No matter what Mom may have prayed for, one can safely assume that when she and Dad went to the family cottage in Essex, Massachusetts, in late September, just weeks following her diagnosis, they both believed with some certainty that they would not be returning, together, in the spring for the ritual "opening" of the cottage for a new season.

For them, Essex (and especially Robbins Island, their special corner of Essex) was hallowed ground. It is where their great love story began. As told by Dad when we were kids—told *many* times because we so loved the way he told the story's exciting denouement—the story begins like this: Soon after he reported for duty as a young intern at Lawrence General Hospital, he was invited by the good Dr. David Wallwork, then chief of surgery, to spend a Saturday at the oceanfront Wallwork cottage on the North Shore of Massachusetts. Some of the senior physicians at the hospital made a point of reaching out to new interns, extending social invitations in order to warmly welcome them to their new medical communities. In my father's instance, he also was being welcomed to a new country, as he had only recently completed his medical studies and exams in his native Germany.

Dad's version of the love story included many facts embellished by him for dramatic effect, as he always enjoyed making his children laugh. One undisputed and unadorned fact is that lobster was served for lunch. Louise Wallwork, the doctor's wife, had thoughtfully planned and prepared a very special meal for the special guest: a first course of clam chowder followed by steamed lobster. Surely the young German doctor would enjoy this quintessential New England treat! Regrettably, the young doctor's strong aversion to seafood (an aversion he described, incidentally, as a serious *allergy* when he graciously declined the delicacies served) had not been known to the Wallworks. Were it not for the fact that young Dr. Sachsse ostensibly swept their daughter and only child off her feet the moment she set eyes on him, the Wallworks might have taken great offense. However, the potentially catastrophic first impression Eckart's reaction to the midday meal could have created was entirely mitigated by the gleam in daughter Nancy's eyes. His disarming charm and charming accent also had mitigating effects that secured him a spot in their hearts in addition to Nancy's.

As Dad's rendition of the story goes, after having been welcomed by Dr. and Mrs. Wallwork upon his arrival, he walked down the long platform leading to the wharf where Nancy, who happened to be entertaining a boyfriend from the Boston area on that particular Saturday, was to be found. As he approached her on the wharf, Dad recalled, Mom took immediate notice of the distinguished-looking, handsome man coming her way. Their eyes met. They greeted each other. And the poor bloke from Boston was sent packing, dumped in favor of a better prospect!

Mom's version of the story wasn't too different on that point; her date was indeed dispatched unceremoniously to whence he had come. And the rest is history, as they say. It was by all accounts—and especially the account my mother herself kept—a whirlwind romance. They fell quickly and wildly in love.

Evidence of this abounds in a treasure trove of diaries, letters, and poems Mom kept in a special envelope, kept safe in a sealed plastic storage bag, kept hidden deep within one of her bureau drawers. She shared it with me a couple years ago, probably so that I would know it existed and could find it if she were no longer around. Inside the plastic bag was a small envelope addressed, "For Linda, Eric, Claudia, Paula," and inside the envelope was the following short letter:

> Dear Linda, Eric, Claudia, Paula,
>
> Perhaps someday, when we are very old or dead and gone, you'll find this packet and go through it. I never had the heart to throw these things away. It's a pretty personal collection—the MEMO book (diary) begins with the day we met, July 15, 1956. If ever you doubted it was "love at first sight," here's documentation to prove it was. You'll see that we were young, hormones raging. You'll see that we were truly, literally young—very, very young, and naïve—"innocent," if you will. (We thought we were worldly-wise.)
>
> It's a great love story. And you were born of it.
>
> I wonder when you'll read this!
>
> Bless you all (you and yours),
>
> Mother

In this packet is a four-page, enchanting letter from Dad, written in his best, but still-not-polished, English and postmarked July 21, 1956 (i.e., less than a week since their first meeting on the wharf), in which he captured his feelings with this bottom-line assessment: "I don't know anything about you except three points: You are Dr. Wallwork's daughter, you are beautiful, and I love you." Mom's four-page answer to the letter, dated July 23, is also in her packet. In response to the young German doctor's declaration of love she wrote, "I should like so much to tell you that I love you. But can love come so fast? I really don't know. If I do not love you, however, why do I think about you constantly, and why do I remember so well every detail of what we said and did on both Sunday and Thursday? Yes, perhaps love *can* come that fast. I think it has come to me."

Mom's diary entries for this period of whirlwind romance include "Something is happening to me . . . and I don't exactly think I want it to" (July 24) and "I honestly think I may be in love" (July 28). By July 29, the matter was settled: "*I love him*. Darn it—I really didn't want this!" On August 14: "Buy 'German Self-Taught' book." She was hooked.

Dad would return many times to Essex (a small fishing town right next to the better-known Gloucester) in the early days of their romance. The cottage had been a favorite spot of my mother's and a source of many great memories for years; her parents had purchased it when she was four. She and her father had caught the huge tuna whose tail hung over the mirror above the fireplace. Just as Gram's hopes of impressing my father with lobster had been dashed, Gramp's hopes of gaining a son-in-law who shared his passion for fishing and his dream that he'd one day haul in "the big one" also were unfulfilled. Not only did my father get squeamish at the prospect of *eating* seafood, especially shellfish, he also wanted nothing to do with the "sport" of snagging one's meal from the dark depths of the big, blue ocean. He became seasick whenever he went out on my grandfather's boat and was queasy when bait, particularly the seaworms we used when bottom-fishing for flounder, was put on hooks. "Waiting for a bite" (often interminably) bored him to distraction. In short, he was no help at all as a fisherman and not much of a companion for the man who became his father-in-law. But both his in-laws fell in love with him almost as quickly as their daughter did, and they adored him (no hyperbole there) for as long as they both lived.

Every summer, my parents would bring our family to Robbins Island in Essex for a two-week vacation. We four children, and eventually our spouses and our children as well, came to love this idyllic spot on Earth as much as my mother did. Each fall, the cozy little cottage needed to be "closed up" and readied for winter before the water was turned off in mid-October. My parents had planned to spend a week in Essex and close up the cottage in September of

2008, by which time the heat and humidity of August would have subsided and we "kids" would all have had our turns for family summer vacations of our own.

My parents' September 2008 week at the cottage turned out to be just a weekend instead. And at one point, they were not sure they would go at all, as it had seemed possible, following Mom's diagnosis on September 8, that the schedule for whatever treatment she might undergo or the side effects of treatment would require her to stay home in Enfield. Mom really wanted to go, but her desire had more to do with a perceived need to say good-bye to dear friends and a special place than with anything else. The trip would be much more about closing a huge chapter of her life than about closing the cottage for winter.

From: Nan & Eck
Sent: Friday, September 19, 2008 6:05 AM
To: Linda Campanella; Eric Sachsse; Claudia S. Barr; Paula Blaker
Subject: ESSEX

MY DEARS, MY SUPPORTERS:
ESSEX WILL BE BEAUTIFUL, WONDERFUL, BUT THESE ARE SURE TO BE MY MOST DIFFICULT DAYS YET. IT WILL BE HARD, AND I FEAR I MAY BREAK DOWN. A PLACE OF SO MANY OF MY HAPPIEST MEMORIES SINCE AGE FOUR. THE PLACE (THE WHARF) WHERE FIFTY-TWO-PLUS YEARS AGO DAD AND I FIRST MET AND YES, I DO BELIEVE, FELL IN LOVE THAT VERY DAY! MAGIC! PLEASE WISH ME COURAGE AND SEND ME ALL YOUR GOOD VIBES!

The weekend in Essex turned out to be, in Mom's words, "a magical weekend." Given the pall that must have hung overhead, I had a hard time believing this, despite the wonderful photos taken of Mom and Dad—smiling, arms around each other, in front of the cottage—and of Mom together with the gal-pals she has known for decades. Somehow my parents had managed to make lemonade out of the lemons, and, in so doing, they (but mostly Mom) set a tone that she and we tried to carry forward throughout the months that followed.

From: Linda Campanella
Sent: Sunday, September 21, 2008 8:16 PM
To: Betty Calder
Cc: Nan & Eck
Subject: FW: Sunset 08

Dear Betty,

I was visiting my parents when your e-mail ("a little slice of heaven") arrived. Heavenly, indeed! I thought you might enjoy the attached slices to go with yours. Robbins Island is, without question, a spot unlike any—as close to heaven as one can come.

And speaking of heaven, my mother was on "cloud nine" when I arrived late this afternoon, shortly after she and Dad had arrived home from Essex. Their weekend on the Island was, as she put it, "magical," and she was just soaring on a magic carpet of happiness as she recalled the past forty-eight hours. I've now seen all the photos and they certainly attest to a good time had by all, especially Mom. It meant so much to her that you made special plans to be there while she and Dad were there to close up our cottage for the season. This mini "reunion" to end the 2008 summer season on Robbins Island and to wish her and my father well on the tough journey they are embarking on was certainly special. She loves you all; you are "the real deal," as she put it—old friends who are truly good friends. I know in my heart she'll be back to open up in the spring; this weekend surely gives her added incentive to fight as hard as she can. She *is* a fighter, and she is so strong. With all the love and support that surround her, she is bound to do well even against tough odds.

Thank you for being the friend you are. It means a lot to me as her daughter.
Love,
Linda

At the celebration of life held in Mom's honor a few days after she died, one of the central displays was a poster entitled "It was a magical year." (Incidentally, Betty and almost *all* Mom's Robbins Island friends (quite a crowd!) drove more than a couple hours in order to be with us at the celebration, something that touched our family deeply and would have made Mom so happy.) Featured on the "magical year" poster were several pictures of Mom laughing with abandon; she had adopted "laughter is the best medicine" as a mantra following her diagnosis and subscribed to it as a way of life for however much life she might have left. She never wanted to lose her sense of humor, and she didn't.

On the table surrounding the poster were framed pictures that portrayed some of the magical moments we experienced during Mom's last year. In the center of the table were two photo albums filled to the gills with photographs taken throughout the year of magic making by our family. Included among the photos are several taken when Mom and Dad returned to Robbins Island in May 2009 to open the cottage for the coming season. Yes, they did! And then, closer to the back of the second album, were more photos of Mom with her gal-pals, these taken when she returned yet again, this time confined to her wheelchair, in early August.

I recall few more exciting or moving developments than that victorious return trip with my parents to open the cottage in May. Claudia joined us, and the four of us made plenty of magic. We went to favorite places, did favorite things, visited with favorite people, and ate favorite foods. With a sense of adventure and good humor, Mom ordered quesadillas off the menu at a new restaurant in Gloucester, announcing with a smile that this was the first time she had ever tried quesadillas. To this day I distinctly remember admiring her and loving her intensely in that moment; she still had the strength and the compunction to seek and celebrate opportunities to do things for the first time, rather than focusing on and fretting over what she might never do again. These were indeed magic moments. Hard as it may be to believe, we were happy, not sad.

When we left the cottage in May, I do not think any of us believed Mom would *not* be back in summer. The fact that she had lived through winter to welcome spring and return to Essex made all of us, and especially Mom, believe that if *this* had been possible, wouldn't *anything* be possible?

When we left, none of us erased the message on the mirror above the fireplace that we had found upon our arrival. I knew it would be there, because Mom had told me about it, and I had been very uneasy about encountering it. At the end of her "magical weekend" back in September 2008, Mom had exited the cottage for what she thought would be the last time; but then she ran back in and hastily wrote a short message, in lipstick, on the mirror for Dad, her children, and her grandchildren to discover after she had died. For a number of reasons, I am very glad we discovered it while she was still with us.

Her words, "Love—always love," still (I am writing this on November 24, 2009) are on the mirror. They are words that capture her essence and describe her life better than any. These words, chosen by Mom instead of any others to be a last message to us, also capture and convey her wish for us. Probably each of us has a slightly different interpretation, or perhaps even multiple interpretations, of what she meant for us to think or do in response; but I'm sure all of us feel her deep and abiding love as we recall these words from her and consider their possible meaning for our lives.

I don't know when any of us, or which one of us, will decide it is time to erase them. "Erasing" is an act that seems especially difficult when one is coming to terms with loss and grief. Dad still has not felt inclined or able to erase the greeting on his answering machine at home; his sweetheart's voice exists in our memories and, more accessibly, on that tape. I experience a surge and complex mix of emotions every time I call and hear the recorded message rather than my father's live voice. I'm not sure exactly how I feel about hearing Mom asking me to please leave a message at the beep, and I can only imagine what Dad is feeling and struggling with as he contemplates whether and when to tape over her voice with his own.

In the packet of love letters and other things Mom saved to share with her children one day, I found historical reminders of why Tchaikovsky's *Swan Lake*, yellow roses, and Chopin had such special meaning to my parents throughout their marriage. I also found a letter written by Mom two months before her wedding in which she said, "Eckart, I don't know why I write all this, when all I really want to say is that I love you. And that I don't know how I ever lived without loving you or without your love, which I need so very much. Life certainly never before had the meaning which it has for me now."

Today, though he does not come right out and say it, I know my father wonders, in the emptiness and loneliness that have descended on him, whether life will ever again have the meaning it has had for him. For fifty-two years, he had his *liebe* Nancy by his side, and now she is gone. But her love lives—in him, through him, around him.

Love—always love.

Living

Calendars

After Mom's diagnosis, several of us in the family, including Mom herself, resolved to "be in the moment" and resist the fast-forwarding our minds were inclined to lapse into when our thoughts were free to wander. This kind of *carpe diem* thinking was very helpful, as it kept grief at bay. However, there was an unhelpful and initially unrecognized liability associated with this strategy. While on the one hand our resolution to not think ahead anesthetized us against pain, the commitment to being "in the moment" also suggested, it seemed to me, a tacit acceptance of and acquiescence in the proposition that for Mom there was no future to look forward to. That was not a particularly motivating scenario. *Let's focus on today because tomorrow may never come . . .* or *because tomorrow my symptoms might incapacitate me and render life as I know it impossible.* We needed a better plan!

I realized it was probably inevitable that my mother would wake up each day and wonder, even if only subconsciously, if today was the day she would turn the corner to her demise and begin to understand in tangible ways the meaning of "terminal." However, or perhaps *therefore*, I began to realize how important it was to balance our "in the moment" strategy with one that anticipated Mom would be around to "seize the day" not just today and tomorrow, but also next week and next month and even next summer.

By early November, less than two months from diagnosis, my mother had completed radiation therapy for her brain metastases and undergone two of four planned chemotherapy sessions to attack the primary lung cancer. We had no idea whether any of this treatment had been effective in shrinking her cancerous growths, but we did know that Mom was not feeling well after the chemo. She was much better than she had feared being—there was no nausea at all—but she still felt really lousy. On November 2, Joe and I brought my visiting in-laws to Enfield for a visit with my parents. Our stomachs were in knots because, despite the optimism we wore on our faces, we believed in our hearts that this would likely be the last time the four of them would be together.

My mother-in-law, Margie, wanted to bring my mother a gift and asked me if I had any ideas. No especially good ideas came quickly to mind, and so we embarked on a stroll through West Hartford Center, anticipating we would recognize a good idea when we saw one. Then, before we had even left the house, it hit me. My mother had always, for as long as I can remember, used a calendar to keep track of upcoming events and commitments and also to serve as a sort of diary or record of past activities and milestones. Margie should give her a 2009 calendar and, in so doing, signal the hopeful expectation that Mom would be here in 2009. Margie was delighted by the idea and picked out a beautiful National Gallery of Art weekly calendar book we both knew Mom would enjoy looking through.

It was in hindsight the perfect gift. Mom was visibly moved by the gesture, and the subtle message behind the gift was not lost on her. In the days, weeks and, yes, months that followed, she and I used the calendar constantly. It helped her think of coming days as new opportunities that she would look forward to and live for, not as passing days that would bring her closer to the day when life would stop. Because for us "terminal" didn't carry with it a termination date *per se*, we could allow ourselves to plan ahead.

And so we did. We looked ahead. We recorded upcoming events, from appointments to birthdays to visits from my sister Paula and family from Washington to days my father would be working at the hospital. And we didn't just record what was already known and scheduled. We also created new plans. At the end of January, Mom, Dad, and I took a trip to visit Claudia and family in New Jersey for a couple days. In March, the three of us went to visit Eric in New Hampshire on the occasion of his daughter Eva's singing a solo in a school performance.

Each time Mom did something adventurous, overcoming her limitations or inhibitions to welcome opportunities and embrace life, we knew we could continue to imagine and plan. The calendar was an instrument of hope and a tool for living. In recording plans, we signaled and affirmed our belief in what was still possible. A diagnosis of terminal cancer does not terminate life. Mom's calendar helped her plan for life rather than plan for death. She kept the calendar by her side and referred to it daily.

As helpful as the calendar was as a life-affirming prop, it was at least equally as helpful and significant in another important way. As I have already written, Mom had used a calendar to plan and organize her life for as long as anyone could remember. When one is diagnosed with cancer and facing death, the sense of being in control of one's destiny quickly begins to erode and, in fact, much control is lost or relinquished. So much of what was once normal or routine in one's life is lost as well. In keeping a calendar, Mom retained both a semblance of control over her own life and a routine daily activity that had largely defined and guided her pre-cancer existence.

Later, as her disease progressed to the point where she was physically impaired and thus limited in her activities, it became even more important to seek ways to help Mom feel as though she was still in control, could still do and decide for herself, and could still participate in the mundane but meaningful routines that had filled her days when she was healthy and planning to live into her nineties.

That 2009 calendar, presented to Mom on November 2, 2008, was a gift that kept giving in ways imagined and unimagined at the time it was unwrapped. Today it is filled with evidence that Mom's last year was a full, and in many ways fulfilled, one.

In reflecting on the year and trying to discern what made it so wonderful while being simultaneously so dreadful, one factor comes repeatedly to mind: We kept believing in what was still possible rather than dwelling on or anticipating what was impossible. Perhaps because her will to live was so strong, Mom kept surprising us and, more importantly, herself with what she could still do. Consequently, she and we never really had a sense that she was doing anything for the last time; there were so many next times that came to pass.

There was an especially memorable trip to Mom and Dad's cottage at Wildwood in the Berkshires in early February. On this occasion, all four of their children (plus a bunch of grandkids) were there. Back in October we had celebrated Mom's seventy-fourth birthday there, thinking (but of course not verbalizing the thought) that it might be her last trip to Wildwood. While we were there, we dared look forward to a family gathering at the cottage for Christmas, as has been family tradition, but I'm sure privately we all feared Christmas might be "celebrated" without the one who loved these big, festive get-togethers more than anyone. It wasn't. All the family, except for Paula and gang in Washington, was together again at the lake for Christmas 2008.

Even that wasn't Mom's last time at Wildwood. The February return trip was followed by a gathering with Paula's whole family at the beginning of April. Claudia, Eric, and I celebrated Mother's Day with her at Wildwood in May. On August 1, which was an absolutely gorgeous summer day, Mom, Dad, Joe, and I made a day trip to Wildwood for a visit with good friend and Wildwood neighbor Bobye List. In addition to wanting to visit with Bobye, who was so incredibly good to Mom and all of us during the year, we wanted to test whether we'd be able to get Mom up onto the deck in her wheelchair, to which she now was confined, and around the corners on the first floor of the cottage. We wanted to confirm Wildwood would be an option for when Paula and family returned for a visit later in the month. Unfortunately, Mom never did make it back to Wildwood for that gathering, but our afternoon on the deck on August 1 was yet again an opportunity to create wonderful memories of good times together.

After Mom's hospitalization in early June following seizures that signaled the disease's progression, she was quite limited in terms of her physical abilities. But even then we didn't stop looking and planning ahead. As summer progressed, we used the calendar less as a planning tool, as we needed to be a bit more impromptu about our outings; but we kept taking them, as the e-mail update to my godmother and Mom's oldest friend below attests:

From: Linda Campanella
Sent: Friday, July 24, 2009 10:49 AM
To: Betty Fitzjarrald
Subject: Good days

Hi, Aunt Betty. We've had a very good week in Enfield, I'm happy to report. Attached as evidence are some photos taken yesterday. Mom looks wonderful and I think she would tell you that she's been feeling pretty darn good, too. We are so grateful.

As you'll see in one of the photos, we are now mobile! Last Saturday I suggested out of the blue (but with my persistent hope/encouragement that we focus on living and injecting life/normalcy/"doing" into the dynamic in Enfield) that Mom, Dad, and I have a little outing—to Burger King for drive-through/take-out lunch. Mom was up for it (she is amazing!), Dad was delighted by the whole idea (one I believe he would never have thought possible), and we did it (with no problem!). What a sense of freedom and new possibilities! Mom used the word "independence" to describe the realization that she is neither bed-bound *nor* home-bound. With that newfound sense of freedom, the next adventure was, believe it or not, a day trip on Monday *to Essex!* Claudia, Dad, and Mom made the trip, and it was super. Mom was able to visit with her Robbins Island friends, and the day was capped off with fried clams at Farnham's! Everyone was so thrilled. Last night, we (Mom, Dad, Eric, B, and I) went to Outback restaurant for dinner, which is where the attached photo was taken.

So that's the update from here. So glad it's a good one! With love to you and Uncle Launy,
Linda

Good days, in ways big and small

If it wasn't divine intervention, it certainly was good luck that I was relatively unencumbered and flexible at the time of my mother's diagnosis. In 2001, I had done what is now commonly referred to as "opting out"; I jumped out of the fast lane—fancy title, fat paycheck, long hours, enviable success, no time for any of the things in life that really matter—and chose to be more present in the lives of my teenage sons, my husband, and also my parents, who lived only a half hour away and both were in good health. I was able to adjust my schedule and my life in order to devote whatever time I wanted or needed to devote to loving, appreciating, and mothering my children at a challenging time in their lives. Now that same flexibility to address personal priorities allowed me to devote myself to supporting my parents at a challenging time in their lives.

Initially I was uncertain what I should do; the sense of foreboding and fear following my father's call was accompanied by a sense of being overwhelmed and helpless. For me this was unsettling, to say the least. The name of my consulting firm is SOS Consulting Group, with SOS standing for "Strategies, Options, and Solutions." Why couldn't I think of any strategies, options, or solutions for Mom? What could I do?

From: Linda Campanella
To: Nan & Eck
Sent: Sunday, September 14, 2008 9:38 AM
Subject: brainstorm!

Guten Morgen,

I have had a brainstorm. A brilliant idea, if I do say so myself. Be open to it ...

As you know, I have periodically had consulting engagements that involved dedicating two days per week to a particular client over an extended period of time. You may not know that I have been hoping to expand my consulting practice into the health care field. Well, not exactly, but ... Something occurred to me. It occurred to me not in the context of my business expansion plan, of course, but in the context of the therapy routine you are about to get into. I was thinking about what good medicine it might be for both of you if Dad could keep working during this period. I was thinking about a lot of related things when it suddenly occurred to me that Dad and I could coordinate calendars so that two days a week I'm "consultant" at 14 Partridge Run, responsible for taking Mom to appointments, etc., and Dad is plugged back into the radiology department work schedule. I have recently finished a bunch of big projects and my fall/winter load is really quite light. I could, without *any* problem, but with much happiness because it would mean I am helping you, devote two days (or more) to a "project" in Enfield. I am only thirty minutes away! This is a blessing. You must let me be helpful, as I am uniquely able, as a family member, now an empty nester, and someone in close proximity, to do this. I think the idea of my planning to be in Enfield on Tuesdays and Thursdays or Mondays and Wednesdays (or whatever schedule makes most sense) during the treatment regimen is both brilliant and logical. It will give you each a break and it will give you, Dad, the chance to be at Baystate Medical Center (BMC) for purposes other than accompanying Mom to chemo or radiation treatments.

Please think about this carefully, both of you. It could work. It is something I *want* to do if it makes sense to and for you. There's a tough road ahead; you will need to learn to say "yes" to offers of help. And mine's *the bestest*.

By the way…don't worry about the expense. I give my long-term clients a very favorable rate.

XOXO

Poo

Mom became my "client," and, thankfully, it was a longer "consulting" gig than either of us imagined.

From: Nan & Eck
Sent: Sunday, September 14, 2008 10:53 AM
To: Linda Campanella
Subject: Re: brainstorm!

Yes, *Guten Morgen*! You are so dear! I absolutely love brainstorms! But you are running way ahead of yourself! Remember, I am living in the moment and one day at a time. TOMORROW will be informative. I may not be a candidate for chemo! And I may decide I prefer two to three weeks of relative comfort as opposed to two to three months of misery. Or I may be told (bullshitted into believing?!) that there's a good chance of improvement and comfort ahead. Who knows? We'll wait and see.

Love and hugs, Mom

From: Linda Campanella
To: Nan & Eck
Sent: Sunday, September 14, 2008 1:36 PM
Subject: RE: brainstorm!

Yes, I'm looking ahead a little, breaking my own "be in the moment" mantra. I'll admit that in the first few days after I got the news, I fast-forwarded way too far and found myself overwhelmed by grief. My emotions went straight to grieving. *That* was running way ahead of myself! In the past few days, I've been able to experience acceptance and hope, not grief. I am looking forward to happy memories, however many of them, still to be made. In that sense, I *am* in the moment. God willing, there will be many, many more memories. I believe there will be.

Yes, I realize tomorrow will be informative. I'll be realistic. But not fatalistic. You asked me not to be "glum." So I am thinking ahead to your treatment, trying to figure out how we might make it as bearable as possible for you two while you go through it and imagining a long, perhaps odds-defying period of remission if not a cure. And meanwhile, we can focus on ways for us all to find joy in every day. This, in a perverse sort of way, may be a "gift" rendered by the diagnosis of cancer. We make every day, every moment, count. I've squandered many in my fifty years, you can be sure!

I will continue to hope and believe (without having to be "bullshitted into believing"!) there's a good chance of improvement and comfort ahead. Just today in the *Hartford Courant* there was a story of a forty-four-year-old who nine years ago was diagnosed with stage-IV colon cancer and given only a slight "chance" of surviving very long at all. Stories like his are out there, and they inspire the hope I believe we all want to have as you take the steps ahead. You have always been a fighter. Remember your mantra: Don't give up!

I do realize, though, that we are taking one day at a time. Who knows what tomorrow will bring. I hope *today* will be a good day for you in some way, big or small.

Always,

Poo

Soon enough, my father did plug himself back into the radiology department schedule at BMC and was out of the house working two or three days each week. On those days, he conducted medicine as a highly esteemed radiologist called out of retirement because he was so good (and because he had made no secret of the fact he was eager to be back at it!). When he was at the hospital in his white coat, Dad's practice of medicine was professional, not personal. He was not married to the patients, and they were not going to die and leave him a widower. It was inestimably good for him to close the door on his house and leave behind, for a day at a time, his role as caregiver doctoring to a terminal cancer patient he happened to adore and assume, instead, the role he was so much happier, not to mention much better equipped, to play.

He was (and remains) excited enough to be working that he would leave the house no later than 5:45 a.m. I would arrive in Enfield by 8:00 a.m., knowing that Mom would have fallen back to sleep if she had even awakened to say good-bye to Dad. I would usually arrive to find a pot of brewed coffee on the counter, Muffet's empty food dish on the floor in front of the dishwasher, and the peel of two clementines in the kitchen sink. Before leaving early each morning, Dad would peel the clementines, position the carefully separated wedges on a saucer, and lovingly place the saucer on his empty pillow for Mom to find when she awoke. Will I ever eat a clementine again without thinking of her and of Dad's love for her? Not likely.

Whenever workdays were added to his schedule, Dad would call or e-mail me to coordinate our calendars. When he worked, I went to Enfield so that Mom would have company and Dad would have piece of mind. "I don't need a babysitter," my mother would say. And she didn't. I didn't let her get away with that kind of talk either. She was persuaded that our days together were at least as much for me as they were for her. We were happy Dad's work schedule (and we credited it, not Mom's cancer, as the precipitating circumstance) created an excuse for mother-daughter days.

Whenever possible, these days were supplemented by evening or weekend visits that often included Joe and at times one or more of our sons, as well. The get-togethers were especially fun when my brother Eric decided on the spur of the moment that he could arrive in Enfield from New Hampshire in time to join us. Eric's special talent and well-honed ability to locate and tickle my parents' funny bones proved invaluable throughout the year. He could be relied upon to lighten the moment with healthy doses of laughter, whose value as "best medicine" is certainly well documented.

The comic relief Eric provided was as important a contribution to the communal care giving by family members as any of the medications Dad administered or the more hands-on relief the three daughters were instinctively more inclined than the son to provide. And my father clearly loved having his only son around—for any reason and on any occasion. Mother-daughter relationships were not the only special bond to have grown firmer during Mom's illness. I think it's possible Eric perceived his most important role during the year to be ministering to our father's needs in ways he was uniquely equipped to do. My sisters and I certainly were attuned and attentive to Dad's needs, but Eric offered something intangible that none of the three of us could tap within ourselves.

Knowing that he could arrive in two hours and bring smiles to everyone's faces, I tried to keep Eric regularly updated on events in Enfield and opportunities to "crash the party," because I also knew he would want to if he could. Paula and Claudia of course wished they lived close enough to be part of these special, but often impromptu, moments. Unfortunately, zip codes and, in Paula's case, time zones rendered it impossible for them to drop everything and head over for happy hour or grilling on the deck or dinner at Outback, one of Dad's favorite local restaurants because of bargain-priced, generous-sized portions of juicy rib-eye steak with all the fixin's.

It became clear that none of us wanted to miss a single thing, a single special moment or memory-in-the-making with our mother. Consequently—but also because Mom loved connecting with everyone—I don't think any gathering did not include a speaker-phone call to whichever of the four children wasn't present so that he, she, we or they could be and feel included.

In the early weeks and months, Mom was a fully functioning cancer patient, able to carry on her life largely as she always had. Her greatest challenge was fatigue that gradually evolved into physical weakness, both attributable to the radiation therapy for her brain lesions and then chemotherapy for the lung cancer. She did a lot of sleeping, and when she slept, I worked (as a consulting practice in this Internet age is largely portable). When she was awake, we talked, we laughed, we lived.

From: Nan & Eck
To: Steve Campanella
Sent: Wednesday, October 08, 2008 4:50 PM
Subject: Re: HI!

OH, SWEET STEVE! WHAT A GREAT E-MAIL ... FOR BOTH OF US! THANK YOU SO MUCH. AS I WRITE THIS, I AM WONDERING WHEN WE WILL SEE YOU NEXT. I HOPE IT WON'T BE TOO LONG FROM NOW. I LOOK FORWARD TO ONE OF THE BEAR HUGS YOU ALWAYS GIVE ME.

CHEMO IS GOING WELL. I THINK I'M A TOUGH OLD BIRD. HAVE NO COMPLAINTS, AT LEAST SO FAR. MOM IS COMING TOMORROW AND WILL TAKE ME, AND THEN WE'LL HAVE ANOTHER MOTHER/DAUGHTER DAY TOGETHER, DAYS THAT ARE SO SPECIAL FOR ME. I AM HAPPY AND BLESSED, AND LIFE IS GOOD. AND YOU ARE ONE OF MY SPECIAL BLESSINGS. ON THAT NOTE, A BIG HUG AND TONS OF LOVE FROM BOTH OPA AND ME.

NAN

On our days together, we always listened to classical music, rediscovering and replaying favorite CDs. We drank tea. We did crossword puzzles (for fun and also to help Mom realize her mind and memory were functioning very well, despite what she might think or fear). We read (though in time this became very difficult for her because of loss of sight in her left eye). We consulted and updated her calendar. We went to appointments, meeting Dad at the oncologist's office every few weeks. We went to CVS to pick up a few items now and then. We planned other quick outings and some longer excursions.

We looked through the American Cancer Society catalogs at scarves, and she phoned to order a few she thought would look good and be comfortable. We went to Barnes & Noble to buy a supply of thank-you cards to send to several friends who already were being so, so good to her; every trip to Barnes & Noble, and there were a few, included a cappuccino or *café au lait* from the Starbucks located inside the bookstore.

One day she told me she wanted to send Halloween cards to her grandchildren, and so we went to the Hallmark store, which she eagerly wanted me to explore with her. She spotted little cartons of mix for mulled apple cider, and to my surprise and indescribable delight, she suggested we get a box because hot mulled cider would be such a nice treat at the Wildwood cottage in winter. *At the Wildwood cottage in winter?* It was mid-October as we were doing our shopping, and Mom was expecting to be around for winter, in two, three, four months. I remember this as though it had happened yesterday; it was the very first time, with me at least, that she had looked that far ahead. Then, for good measure so we would not run out, she suggested we put a second carton in our basket!

As Christmas approached, we made a project of going through a big carton in her basement that contained things she had purchased, accumulated, and saved over the years in order to have a reservoir of gifts to give in the future. Now seemed as good a time as any to start giving those gifts. What a collection it was! We found things for every member of the family—all adults plus eleven grandchildren ranging in age from eleven to twenty-two. We also found a few things she thought her neighbor and friend Doris would like to donate to the Senior Center as well as a couple things for Doris herself!

On a few of my subsequent visits to Enfield, we spent time wrapping the gifts. This was a poignantly difficult thing to do. Mom, who always was famous for wrapping gifts to perfection, was now quite limited in terms of what she could usefully do with her hands. Writing had become a challenge almost immediately after her diagnosis. Slowly other things became more difficult. Cutting wrapping paper and fitting it snugly around packages just was not going to happen this Christmas season. Her "assignment," therefore, was to tear off the pieces of tape we needed to secure the packaging, and she applied the tape wherever I pointed. I thought it was important that family members see her handwriting on the gift tags, so she did her very best to write "To [So-and-So] from Nan and Opa." This was a tough challenge, but she was such a good sport. Quite a few tags were discarded; she needed a do-over. Though we smiled our way through it, with Christmas carols playing in the background, inside my heart was breaking just a little more.

We made gift bags for a group of Autumn Field neighbors as well as for old friends in Longmeadow. She and Dad had purchased special jams at the Granville Store on the way home from our October family reunion at the Wildwood cottage. And soon after that, Mom, Dad, and I had gone together one Sunday afternoon to a store that sells beautiful hand-painted Polish pottery. There she found little jam pots to accompany the jars of jam and various other lovely gifts that she selected thoughtfully with various special people in mind. For Betty in Maine and Longmeadow friend Joan, both of whom are tea drinkers, Mom found an adorable teapot/teacup combination that was wrapped and delivered to each with a note from Mom expressing the hope that, when she was gone, they would think of her whenever they drank tea from these cups. This was another poignant and sad moment for me. Mom kept smiling.

We went for a manicure in the fall in between chemo treatments for a little mood boost. In winter, thanks to Eric's girlfriend Jen, we enjoyed massages at a spa in New Hampshire—Mom's first massage ever. She loved it! I had reassured her before we were ushered to our respective and adjoining rooms that she should feel no pressure to carry on a conversation with Lisa, the masseuse; rather, she should close her eyes and her mouth and do her best to indulge completely in the peaceful relaxation she would experience. Three minutes into my massage, I heard chatter and laughter coming through the walls, and it didn't stop!

I think Mom and Lisa must have gabbed for the entire hour. They emerged smiling, bosom buddies. A special bond had been formed during their time together. This was obvious to me in the heartfelt best wishes Lisa extended with moist eyes as we left; she clearly had been touched by Mom and her buoyant spirit. My impression was confirmed a week later when Mom received a sweet note in the mail from Lisa. I have a hard time imagining too many people who would inspire their massage therapist to make the effort to follow up in this way. Mom had a uniquely engaging and generous way of connecting with people and, without ever setting out to do so, she would win their friendship.

In her illness, Mom shed not only her hair but also her inhibitions, self-consciousness, and any exterior protective screen. One enjoyed a clear view of her inner beauty and a direct route to her huge heart, her authentic self. She was arguably never more lovely, loving, or lovable than in her last year.

On a hot day in May, we sat side by side for a pedicure. She was still strong enough to walk, using her walker, from the car to the nail shop. The pedicurist doing Mom's toes said he thought we were sisters. Under other circumstances, I might have been a little perturbed; I was feeling old enough as it was, thank you very much. On that day, it was all about Mom, and I was so happy to be described as her sister. We were soul sisters, for sure. And she did appear young, healthy, and stylish; she was wearing a cute new blouse from

Marshall's, her hair looked super, she had the feet and calves of a much younger woman, and she was in great spirits. Neither pedicurist could believe the hair was a wig. Feeling she needed to resort to drastic measures to make her point, but mostly feeling impish, Mom whipped off the wig to show her hairless head. She was fabulous!

The new shirt from Marshall's was one of quite a few recent additions to her closet. The last thing Mom *needed* was new clothes; someday, when Dad feels ready to give away Mom's belongings (and of this writing the day has not come yet), the Salvation Army or Big Brothers/Big Sisters will receive quite a bounty! Question of need or no need aside, earlier that month (May), I decided it would be fun to refresh her wardrobe with some new summer tops; this was less about clothes and shopping than it was about hope and living. I liked the idea of looking forward a couple months and giving her the opportunity to express the expectation she would be around to sweat through summer by buying clothes for it. It was also important, I thought, for her to realize and affirm that it still felt good to look good. I brought her a dozen options, purchased one afternoon while she napped, and we had a blast trying them on and picking which to keep, which to return. I was delighted when, on a future visit to Enfield, she was waiting for me with a pile of catalogs, all with dog-eared pages that featured possible purchases; she had been going through the catalogs and found quite a few additional things she thought she might like to have on hand for summer. Hooray!

My goal for most of the year was to help Mom (and to some extent Dad, as well) feel life as she had known and lived it did not stop on September 8, 2008, and believe that "normalcy" could prevail even under circumstances that felt anything but normal. It was important for them and us to keep doing what we had always done, even if we had to go about doing it differently to accommodate a "new normal." Every day I spent in Enfield I tried to find a reason for Mom to leave the house with me to "do" something—so that she would feel, at the end of the day, as though she had in fact done something and was not confined to her house and a shrinking world. We made quite a few trips to RiteAid to develop photos taken to commemorate fun family gatherings or visits from good friends; the photo counter attendant always remembered her and, like the massage therapist Lisa, had become a buddy.

Even when she no longer had the strength to walk the aisles herself, I would bring her with me to Big Y, after first putting our heads together and jointly developing a short shopping list. She and Muffet, who always loved going for rides, would sit in the parking lot while I ran in to buy a few things for her fridge, something to whip up for dinner, or new African violets to replace the ones on her kitchen window sill that had died because no one other than Mom ever watered them, and she hadn't watered them in ages because she couldn't reach the sill from her wheelchair.

We'd go to Dunkin' Donuts and enjoy chit-chat over a cup of coffee sitting at a table inside; later, when she was weaker and not walking more than the distance from her house to the car in the driveway, we'd get our java at the Dunkin' drive-through window and carry on our conversation in the car while tooling about town. A couple times, we drove to Longmeadow, through the old neighborhood, past the house on Park Drive, by the church where my sisters and I were married, and other familiar landmarks that always provided fodder for reminiscences and conversations. We'd periodically stop at Blockbuster Video and, while she and Muffet sat waiting, I'd run in and pick a few movies for Dad and her to enjoy or for the two of us to watch later in the day while Dad was working.

We filled our days with as much activity as made sense on a particular day, and each day was a little different. As Mom became weak from treatments, Dad was much more inclined than I to not "push" her to do things. He wanted her to be comfortable and happy, and if she said she was tired or had no energy, he would take that declaration at face value and believe it best for her that she rest. He'd sometimes, somewhat reflexively, say "No" to a suggestion from me regarding something we might do, only to have Mom chime in with her own opinion: in fact she *could* do such-and-such and would actually *like to*. I kept pushing, feeling confident that she would push back if she really didn't want to or simply couldn't do something being suggested.

Though there were many times when she absolutely needed to succumb to her weakness and fatigue, and indeed insisted on doing so, there were just as many times when she was eager and able to muster the enthusiasm, if not the energy, necessary to say yes to an opportunity presented her. Where there was a will, she found a way, and we did so much on our days together that surprised the hell out of Dad when he came home from work and received a report of our day.

Mom had good days and bad days during her last year. The good days were sometimes good in small ways, other times in big ways. She had happy hours and she had a few not-so-happy moments. On balance, though, the good and the happy far outweighed the not good and sad. Looking back, I see so much joy. Truly, there was joy in every day. In spite of the sad context in which life was being lived, life was lived joyfully.

During that year of my "consulting" in Enfield, countless wonderful memories were created—memories that now, in her absence, provide regular reminders of my extraordinary mother and the special bond we forged. We did so many things together that it is, quite simply, impossible for me go through a day without hearing, seeing, smelling, eating or doing something, or going someplace that connects me with Mom. Our lives became so intertwined that I feel she is a part of me and my own everyday existence. The list of things that make me think of her is seemingly endless, and for that I am endlessly thankful. Even when the reminders make me sad, I am thankful. Increasingly the memories make me smile, and for that I am even more thankful.

Linda Campanella

Happy hour

Looking back on the year and a day following Mom's diagnosis and thinking about why this time was filled with so much happiness despite miserable circumstances and poor prognoses, one thing comes immediately to mind: happy hour! Happy hour became one of the "signature" events and defining experiences of Mom's "magical" last year. It became something akin to either religion or addiction. We practiced it faithfully, and we experienced withdrawal if we went too long without.

Happy hour, and sometimes just anticipation of happy hour, lifted our spirits when they needed lifting. (When *didn't* they need lifting?) Happy hour could be plugged into any or every day if we felt like it. We needed happy hour. We didn't need it in the way an alcoholic needs his drink. We needed it because on the inside, none of us was happy; we were heartbroken because we knew Mom's days (and thus happy hours) were numbered. Happy hour came to be an oasis of joy in a desert of despair.

Even on what were "bad days" for Mom, we could manage to have a "happy hour" or two, sitting around the living room fireplace or the patio table and just being together—talking, sharing, and always finding reason to laugh and feel happy…authentically so. We did not have to manufacture or fake happiness. Happy hour did not command happiness; it permitted happiness. Happiness just happened.

I introduced happy hour very early in the year, as soon as I began spending days in Enfield with my mother while Dad worked at the hospital. I was distraught, not happy, in those early days, but I had resolved to help Mom find joy in every day. This was my self-appointed mission. If there was joy in every day, I told myself, Mom would be motivated to muster whatever will or strength she needed in order to fight the good fight, believing she could have many more good days than predicted. This is what I wanted desperately, so I did what I could to make her days good days, her hours happy hours.

With our first happy hour—wine, crackers, cheese, gas fire ablaze, piano concerto piped through the speaker system into the living room—Mom and I welcomed Dad home from work at the hospital. We asked him about his day and told him about ours. He was visibly thrilled to see Mom in such good spirits. In the days and weeks that followed, I believe he, more than anyone else, looked forward to happy hour. He would walk through the door from work and know it had been an okay day for his sweetie pie if she was in good enough shape to be sitting in the wing chair next to the fireplace or out on the deck waiting for him to join us and tell us about his day.

Happy hour was something to look forward to later in a day that might not have started too well. It was a something to "do" on days that, for Mom, were no longer filled with much activity or excitement. Mom could still "do" happy hour even when she could not do much else. There were days when Mom did not get out of bed or dressed except for happy hour. On those days, I think she motivated herself for Dad's benefit largely, because she knew he used happy hour as a barometer to gauge how well she was doing, and she knew how much these moments of celebrating life meant to him.

Eventually, we extended happy hour to days of the week when Dad was not working; we did not need his coming home from work as an excuse to uncork a bottle of wine and pull out the Triscuits and Cabot cheese. Dad started buying Triscuits in volume (whenever they were on sale). He was delighted whenever Big Y promoted

Cabot cheese with a special offer (buy one, get two free!) and was tickled when Joe and I could get Jarlsberg for $3.99 a pound at Stew Leonard's. He asked Joe to pick out some good wines at our favorite wine shop in West Hartford (where we had always had good luck finding very nice wines in the $10 a bottle range); he wanted us to bring him a case so he would always have a ready supply. Throughout the year, Joe would periodically be asked to restock the supply, always to be reimbursed by Dad, who was beginning to develop a fondness for a few of the finer Cabernets.

But happy hour was not about the wine or the beer. We didn't drink much at all. Happy hour was about the act of setting aside a time of day to celebrate life and each other. We would celebrate with a bottle of beer or a glass of wine to accompany our cheese and crackers and, in doing so, make the hour more legitimately a happy hour in the traditional sense. If Eric was to be part of the gathering, Dad would stock up on beer and peanuts—Eric's idea of happy hour treats. Whenever Claudia was in town, happy hour's offerings looked rather different than the meager munchies I thought sufficed; Claudia, being the fabulous cook and hostess extraordinaire that I am not, served up far more elaborate and elegant hors d'oeuvres that added flare (and flavor) to the fun. Paula enjoys red wine as much as I do, and whenever we overlapped for a happy hour in Enfield, we invariably discovered one of us had walked off with, and finished, the other's glass of wine.

These truly were fun times. Happy hour made our abnormal existence feel normal. Happy hour also provided a mechanism for expanding Mom's shrinking world, an existence in which direct human contact was limited on most days to members of her immediate family. Mom always was a very social person who loved interacting with people and cherished close friendships. While she enjoyed phone conversations with friends during her illness, these conversations were no substitute for time together face to face. So why not invite folks to join her for happy hour if she was up for a visit? That's just what we did occasionally, and these were fun times as well. Bittersweet, but the dominant and lasting feeling such get-togethers evoked was one of joy. Good people were having a good time, living in the moment, and loving life.

Just as tenaciously as Mom seemed to be holding on to life, I held on to happy hour. *None* of us wanted to give it up because doing so would feel like giving up … giving up on living, on hope, on Mom. If she could still get out onto the deck for happy hour, life was still good.

> From: Linda Campanella
> Sent: Wednesday, June 17, 2009 5:48 PM
> To: Eric Sachsse
> Subject: RE: A beautiful day on the deck in Enfield!
>
> Yesterday at 4:30, Mom had awakened and I was visiting with her in bed. By then, Dad, Paula, and I had decided on happy hour on the deck. Dad came in to check on Mom and asked her if it was okay if the three of us had happy hour for ten minutes. In that moment, my heart broke a little more. We were about to have happy hour without her, leaving her alone and awake in her bed. Dad left and I decided to ask if she'd like to join us. She said *yes*, but that she also wanted to stay in bed and sleep more! We chuckled and chatted a bit, and she eventually decided to get up. It was *wonderful*. Plus, she had better strength in legs and on left side generally. Today we did the same thing at lunchtime. I honestly think Dad believed yesterday morning that Mom would never see the deck again. He cried repeatedly during happy hour—because he was happy/sad. His heart was lifted, but still it was/is so heavy.
> XOX
> LSC

Quite a few photos taken at happy hour (and we took many, to document and share with others the fact that Nan was living, and sometimes livin' it up!) show Dad wearing his "Life Is Good" T-shirt. It was a favorite of his, but I think subconsciously he chose to reach for that shirt in the drawer more often than he chose other options because its message proclaimed something he either needed to be reminded of or simply wanted to believe. Happy hour continued until the last days of Mom's life. She joined us for the last time on August 31. Soon thereafter, she slipped into the comatose state in which she would remain until she died on September 9. In the photo taken to memorialize that last happy hour, Dad's T-shirt says "Life Is Good," but the anguished look on his face says otherwise.

We have found the courage and strength to continue happy hour even though someone is missing. The first happy hour and probably the next one or two with Dad alone were difficult. But we leaned into the sadness and came out the other side feeling all right. We did it. I believe Mom would be happy about this, especially since her dying wish was that we not be sad. Happy hour is no time to be sad.

In much the same way we needed to allow ourselves and create opportunities to be and feel happy after Mom's diagnosis and throughout a journey taking us somewhere we didn't want to go, we also needed to do these things after she died. We are developing new habits in response to yet another new normal. I have made a point of going to Enfield at least one day a week on a day when Dad is working so that he can come home to a house that is not empty, save for beloved Muffet. I arrive shortly before he is due to come home. When he walks through the door, he finds the lights are on, the fireplace is ablaze, classical music is playing softly, the cheese and Triscuit platter is ready, and there is someone waiting to ask him, over a glass of Cabernet, how his day was.

LINDA CAMPANELLA

Voodoo medicine

During my mother's ordeal, she endured tests, treatments, side effects, anxieties and indignities of the sort that ordinarily—for ordinary people, that is—lead either quickly or eventually to despair and self-pity. But in her case, they led to neither. As she had written to my son Steve in early October, she was a "tough old bird"! She took it on the chin and kept her chin up. One thing, and really *only* one, caused her frustration and, on rare occasion, led her to feel down enough to unload a complaint. This one thing was, as she put it, her "lack of oomph."

She experienced virtually no symptoms from her cancer, and the most dreaded side effects of chemo never materialized. Not sidelined by the disease or by debilitating nausea, she was eager and able to remain fairly active. Before long, though, the combination of radiation therapy, chemotherapy, and weaning off of steroids had knocked her out of the ring; she was wiped out. Our "doing, not dying" approach to living required oomph, and she had none.

On one of her visits in the fall, my sister Claudia coordinated the purchase of a recliner chair (which not only glided its occupant back into a reclined position, but also could lift and launch her into a standing position). The terrific new chair replaced an old one in the master bedroom and soon became a favorite resting spot for Mom, a place where she could indulge her lack of oomph but still be, technically, out of bed. Whenever I was in Enfield, my goal was to get Mom out of bed *and* out of her bedroom so that she could feel like she was doing, not dying. At times, I felt very frustrated that the recliner seemed to be consigning Mom to an inactive and isolated existence in her bedroom. In 20/20 hindsight we wish the chair had not been procured quite so soon (but who knew then that Mom would live and be quite active for many more months?) and wish it had not been placed in the bedroom (the farthest corner of the house, where one is isolated from activity and other people).

By late fall, Mom's days consisted largely of sleeping in her bed or reclining (and dozing) for hours in her recliner. It took a lot of effort, on both her part and mine, to inject any "doing" into our days together. She was both comfortable in her recliner and too tired to do much at all, even if she were to launch herself out of it. Nevertheless, I made it a point each day I was there—until the very end, in fact—to encourage Mom to get dressed. Most people, and she proved no exception, feel more energetic, more alive, if we are not wearing PJs or a bathrobe; and we feel better if we look good. Unless she truly was too tired to do anything, even get out of her robe, I would help Mom get dressed into an outfit I'd ask *her* to pick (so that *she* was still more or less in control of the mundane matters of her life). Next, a matching cap or scarf would be selected. And then, of course, the final touches. On my days in Enfield, Mom was almost never without earrings or lipstick. Both made her look and feel more alive, more like her old self, lovely.

Sometimes Mom didn't get dressed and primped until a half hour before Dad was due to come home from work. She would tap the few ounces (or drops) of oomph she had and we would ready ourselves for what, on some days, would be our only "activity"—happy hour with Dad. Invariably Dad's spirits would be lifted if he came home to discover Mom waiting for him, cheese and crackers on the coffee table, and a bottle of wine already open on the kitchen counter.

Linda Campanella

Outings with Mom were increasingly few and far between in late fall and early winter. When we did go out, with or without a specific destination, it was always important for her to bring her pocketbook, even if (as increasingly became the case) she had absolutely no need for it. The pocketbook was important not for what purpose it served, but rather for the message it sent to her. It said, *I am still the woman I was.* A woman's pocketbook is, for all intents and purposes, an extension of herself. With her pocketbook on her shoulder or in her lap, Mom was "whole." She was herself and she was ready; she was in control. Like many women, my mother had quite a few bags—options for different types of events, different outfits, different seasons. She had always carried a carefully selected, carefully packed pocketbook containing things she knew she would need (wallet, house keys, lipstick...) as well as whatever she felt she might need and should have with her just in case (tissues, cough drop, sunglasses, pen, cell phone...). Why should she give up carrying her pocketbook even though she often didn't even get out of the car when we went somewhere?

In early December, Mom's oncologist, whom she had been seeing every three weeks or so since treatment started, expressed his belief that her lack of oomph was the result of a combination of factors. (He mentioned specifically the combination of the malignancy, chemotherapy, steroid regimen, and colitis, which was a pre-existing condition.) He lamented that it was impossible to pinpoint which of these was most to blame. He offered no quick energy fixes but did agree with my parents that continuing chemotherapy beyond the two rounds Mom had undergone didn't make sense at this time. "When you're in a hole, stop digging," he admonished. According to an e-mail I sent my folks after this appointment, the doctor also indicated that moving, being upright, and fighting the lack of oomph were things he hoped she would find the will and strength to do, as they were apt to accelerate her rebound from what he surmised were most likely the effects of a too-quick withdrawal from steroids.

In the weeks that followed, Mom did not seem to rebound much at all. She was exhausted and weak. Although the digging had stopped, she had not been able to climb out of the hole. It was exceedingly discouraging to us all that life could be fairly normal for my mother if only she had the energy to live it! Couldn't *something* be done to help her, to give her a boost of energy? The clock was ticking, and precious time was being wasted.

From: Linda Campanella
Sent: Wednesday, January 21, 2009 4:50 PM
To: eckart sachsse
Subject: Idea

Dad, Do not automatically say *no* without considering the following (though I readily admit the idea may be a non-starter)! Should we ask Dr. Hetzel about acupuncture as a possible treatment for chronic fatigue following chemotherapy? I have been reading quite a bit about this (an example is cut and pasted below). Sloan-Kettering is doing a phase III clinical trial (click *here* for a link), I believe.
 Sounds rather promising. Nothing else seems to be helping on the energy-boost front.
 LSC

Had it not been obvious that Mom desperately needed more energy if she was going to be able to live more fully while she was still asymptomatic, I do not think my father—a physician trained in "traditional" medicine and always somewhat skeptical of homeopathic and other non-Western, non-"traditional" approaches to health and healing—would have been as open to and supportive of the idea of acupuncture as he turned out to be. Perhaps he responded to the idea as husband, not as physician. As husband, he was as desperate as the rest of us to find anything that would make Mom feel and function better.

From: Linda Campanella
Sent: Thursday, January 22, 2009 12:23 PM
To: 'info@clinic.com'
Subject: acupuncture for chemo-related fatigue

Dear Sir,

My mother is terminally ill with lung cancer that metasta-
sized to her brain. She has undergone radiation for the brain
tumors and did two rounds of chemo for the primary lung
tumors; then she stopped because the side effects, principally
fatigue, were not bearable. She continues to be symptom-free
from her cancer but her quality of life is severely compro-
mised by what she describes as total "lack of oomph." Because
I believe my mother has the potential to live for months and
because I would like as much of her remaining time to be
"quality time," I have been exploring via the Internet the potential for acupuncture to address fatigue effectively. I am interested to know if you have had any experience with chemo
patients seeking relief from debilitating fatigue and what
course of treatment you might suggest my mother consider
if indeed acupuncture might be a route to take. Thank you.

Linda Campanella
West Hartford

From: Matt , L.Ac.
Sent: Thursday, January 22, 2009 1:29 PM
To: Linda Campanella
Subject: Re: acupuncture for chemo-related fatigue

Hi Linda,

Thanks for getting in touch and for considering acupuncture as a treatment for your mother's fatigue. Acupuncture
(and Chinese herbs) are very effective treatments for the
side-effects of chemo and radiation. In fact, since Chinese
medicine operates from a core philosophy of "energy" as a

basic component of health, it is particularly well-suited to treating fatigue.

Having worked with and helped people in your mother's position before, I would be happy to assist her in feeling better if she decides to go the Chinese medicine route.

Thanks and best wishes,
Matt

From: Linda Campanella
Sent: Thursday, January 22, 2009 2:27 PM
To: 'Matt L.Ac.'
Subject: RE: acupuncture for chemo-related fatigue

Dear Matt,

Thanks for your prompt and positive reply. Just one quick follow-up question for clarification: My mother's second and last round of chemo was over two months ago, so the fatigue she's experiencing is potentially a long-term side effect but not one associated with a current and continuing chemo regimen. I assume your treatment of cancer-/chemo-related fatigue is not linked specifically or directly to chemo that is in process at the time of treatment. In other words, what has worked in treating fatigue in patients who are undergoing chemo is expected to work in patients who underwent chemo recently but stopped some time ago. Is that correct?

Linda

From: Matt L.Ac.
Sent: Thursday, January 22, 2009 2:59 PM
To: Linda Campanella
Subject: RE: acupuncture for chemo-related fatigue

Hi Linda,

That's exactly right. In fact, with Chinese medicine, it doesn't matter what the fatigue is due to (i.e., it could be from chemo or from just running a marathon) - what matters is how the fatigue is expressing itself from a Chinese medicine standpoint (i.e., what organs are affected? which acupuncture meridians are affected? etc.).

Matt

Based on my limited investigation, acupuncture seemed to represent a viable option; not a sure thing, but certainly a safe bet. My sister Paula, a physical therapist, chimed in with a supportive and encouraging voice; unbeknownst to me or my parents, she had undergone acupuncture for a neck injury unsatisfactorily addressed by traditional physical therapy over a three-year period. She reported that despite being both skeptical and pessimistic, she succumbed to a friend's pressure and tried acupuncture; to her surprise and delight, she experienced "incredible results" after only two visits and "lasting results" after five or six. "I wish I understood it more but strongly recommend it (with someone who has experience and good client feedback)," she wrote. "Sounds like Nan has nothing to lose and the potential for positive results. P.S. The needles are painless, almost as thin as hair."

A former radiology colleague of my father's highly recommended an acupuncturist with "experience and good client feedback" when he learned that we were considering the possibility of acupuncture. In fact, this colleague drove straight over to Enfield and took my parents to the acupuncturist's office. And so began our relationship with Dr. Chou and what my father derisively but also with intended humor referred to as "voodoo medicine."

Mom was optimistic and moderately excited. I was totally psyched! Even if the acupuncture did not, in the end, do much to restore my mother's energy, she and I would have something new to do; something to put on the calendar; something that would get her out of the house; something for which she would need her pocketbook! In checking Mom's 2009 calendar for a record to refresh my memory, I found ten appointments between end of February and end of April; she missed one or two because she wasn't feeling up to going, but we went to the rest. And these were fun outings.

Whether it was real acupuncture benefit or placebo effect, Mom seemed to feel some oomph coming back. She had enough energy to travel to Vermont in March for granddaughter Eva's concert. She and I hosted a "Spring Tea in Autumn Fields" for four of her oldest friends on March 30. Paula and her family visited at the beginning of April and the timing was perfect, because Paula could–and did–work with Mom on a regimen of strengthening exercises, which Mom welcomed and which might reinforce whatever good the "voodoo medicine" was doing. There also were a couple days up at the Wildwood lake house. And after that, it was time to plan a trip to Essex to open up the cottage for summer.

From: Linda Campanella
Sent: Monday, April 06, 2009 11:40 AM
To: Bobye List
Subject: You are too much!

Hi, Bobye. I am in Enfield today while Dad works a half day at the hospital.

Our weekend at Wildwood was terrific. As you may know already, Paula, Scott and kids are visiting from Washington. They arrived on Wednesday afternoon and will depart Sunday morning. We (Mom and Dad, Blakers, Joe and I, Eric, Jen and B) headed to the lake for a couple days of bad weather but good times. Mom has been feeling quite good lately; though we can't pinpoint the reason, we assume it is some combination of prednisone to attack infiltrates in her lungs that are a chemo side effect, 24/7 oxygen following congestive heart failure a month or so ago, and acupuncture for the past six weeks, give or take. Her energy level and enthusiasm have returned, although today she is not feeling well and remains in bed as I type this from her computer.

Honestly, although we hoped against hope, none of us was too optimistic she would live to enjoy spring fever and the likelihood of enjoying summer sunsets on the deck at Wildwood and the porch at her beloved Robbins Island (Essex, MA cottage). Though she still carries on "day to day" (as each new day is unpredictably different in terms of how she feels), she definitely is looking forward—farther than she had expected would be on the horizon for her.

I find myself overwhelmed with a sense of gratitude these days—grateful for so many good memories that we have been making these past months. We've all gotten pretty good at being "in the moment." Though we know what lies ahead, it's not in the present; it's not even imminent. So I keep my sadness at bay. It rolls in sometimes, and I indulge it.

I hope you and yours are doing well. Perhaps you'll all be together for Passover. I hope whatever you do it will be special.

With love, thanks, and all good wishes,
Linda

From: Nan & Eck
To: Judy Riggs
Sent: Sunday, May 03, 2009 10:02 PM
Subject: Re: Essex

Dear Judy,

Speaking of Essex and summer, we hope very much we can spend a long weekend or somesuch there in mid-summer, but that is iffy. Indeed, we *do* hope to be there the weekend of May 16 and 17, and at least part of the week that follows. However, this too is now iffy. About a week ago, I was feeling very short of breath (and fatigued by doing nothing), so the pulmonologist ordered a CT scan of the chest. Unfortunately, it showed that the lung tumor has grown, and that there is pleural effusion, which is crowding the lung. So another X-ray late this week will doubtless determine if it's the cancer or the fluid which is giving me problems. Then it will be determined if I should try radiation to the lung or needle aspiration of the fluid... or just wait and see for a while longer. This is why last week was not great and why Essex in May is now iffy. If I am having radiation at that time, it's out. I am, however, crossing my fingers that we'll make it. Please cross yours for us!

I am royally spoiled here by friends and neighbors, and especially by Eckart and all my family. Eckart is truly my caretaker and does just about everything for me. Linda comes two to three times a week, is always here when Eck is working, and she, too, takes over for me, and also gets me to do things I don't really feel like doing (manicure, pedicure!) without her prodding... But she is gentle and kind and doesn't push. We also laugh a heck of a lot. About a month ago, she also coaxed me into having a tea party for some old friends from the neighborhood where our kids grew up (still my best friends from this area) and it was lovely and a great success. Yesterday she and Joe dragged us to see *The Soloist* at an easy-access theater in West Hartford. So there is still a lot of fun in my life.

Two days after the tea party, Paula and family arrived and spent a week here with us... a wonderful week and it was very empty and lonely after they left. Claudia often comes also, more often than she should, considering the long drive. Billy and Brian are now in Haiti for a week doing volunteer work, and Claudia will come here Tuesday for a few days. Eric also comes for a short stay pretty often, sometimes with B and sometimes with both B and Jen. If I am up for it, there will be a family gathering at our lake cottage next weekend.

Love, Nancy

We did gather at the cottage that next weekend for Mother's Day, which came eight months and two days after Mom's diagnosis. While surely we had hoped it, I suspect none of her children believed back then that there would be another Mother's Day with our mother. In calculating what to believe, we had underestimated her strength and did not fully factor in her will to live or her capacity to live joyfully in spite of what her life had become.

A good friend at Essex said several times during the year, when we found ourselves marveling at Mom's steely determination and defiantly upbeat attitude, "She's just not ready to leave the party yet." Perhaps it was that simple.

Day bed

At 7:15 a.m. on May 27, Mom called me to report she had fallen face-first onto the marble hearth in the living room; she said she was okay but bleeding from her nose and mouth. I was ready but hadn't left home yet to join her for the day while Dad worked at the hospital, and she wanted me to call him there and ask him to come home right away. She no longer could remember the phone number in the radiology department and had not been able to find it among the numbers programmed into her phone. I reached Dad immediately after hanging up, but he was about to begin a complicated procedure and simply could not leave in that moment. I told him I could and would. I jumped into the car and made it to Enfield in half an hour, despite the rush-hour traffic.

Unable to get up, Mom had dragged herself on the floor from the living room into her bedroom, where she could reach up and grab a portable phone on the little table next to her recliner chair. When I arrived, she was lying on the floor with dried blood around her swollen nose and under a fat lip. I examined her and found a gash inside her upper lip but no additional or more serious injury except possibly a broken nose. I propped a big pillow under her head and we sat together on the floor, as I was unable to lift her into the chair; we kept each other company, chatting until Dad came home an hour or so later. In surprisingly good spirits in spite of her circumstances, she explained that she had no clue what had happened. She did not know why or how she had made her way from the kitchen, without her walker, to the fireplace. The last thing she could remember was pouring herself a cup of coffee, and this recollection was corroborated by the presence of her walker in the kitchen, standing without her by the counter where her coffee cup rested.

Although we did not know it at the time, this unexplained episode was a turning point, heralding the fact that Mom's brain lesions had multiplied and were growing in ways that would cause seizures. A grand-mal seizure came four days later while Dad was with her; she had complained of a severe headache and was in bed when she started shaking uncontrollably. Dad called me to report that something seemed to be terribly wrong, and then he called 911. She was taken by ambulance to Baystate Medical Center, and somehow Joe and I, coming from West Hartford, managed to beat the ambulance. We were there to greet Dad when he stepped out of the front seat, clearly shaken. We learned later that, en route, he had been asked from the back of the ambulance, where Mom was being attended to, "Is she DNR?" The question jarred him into realizing how serious things were and that he might lose her then and there.

The "reality check" sank in more deeply, for all of us, in the days that followed. Mom's weeklong hospitalization was physically and emotionally exhausting for everyone but for Dad in particular. Mom was not in good shape and her prospects were unknown. This scared the hell out of my father and made him profoundly sad. Eric, Claudia, and I understood implicitly that while it was Mom in the hospital bed, it was Dad who needed our support now more than ever before. We were by his side for the duration, and Paula was with us all in spirit, having been persuaded that she might be more helpful to Dad and also to Mom if she were to delay her coming until after Mom was home again.

Slowly Mom emerged from what was essentially a coma-like state caused by a combination of seizure trauma and medications to control ongoing seizure activity; but she did not emerge totally herself. The anti-seizure drugs caused severe hallucinations that were alarming to both her and us. When she wasn't hallucinating, she was often anxious and agitated, certain that family members were gathered around her because she was going to die. We reassured her constantly and lovingly that she was doing well, seemed to be getting stronger, and would be going home very soon.

I'm not sure Mom had believed our reassurances that she would be going home soon until her discharge orders were signed. By then we had been advised by her primary care physician that we would be wise to begin hospice care, so Mom was discharged with orders to commence a relationship with Home and Community Health Services. An MRI of Mom's brain had revealed a total of eleven growths, one of which was suspected of causing profound left-side weakness and at least one of which was the culprit behind seizure activity that would have to be controlled by carefully monitored, frequently adjusted levels of medication. A chest X-ray revealed pleural effusion that had required insertion of a tube through her chest wall into her pleural cavity so that the accumulating fluids could be drained regularly to relieve pressure. We had arrived at an entirely new level of care.

At the same time, we had reason to believe Mom's visual and auditory hallucinations would continue to taper off and eventually stop following a switch from one anti-seizure drug to another. We were advised by the neurologist that the seizures could in fact be controlled. Resumption of steroids would relieve pressure in the brain, which in turn should help Mom regain some strength and coordination on her left side.

In short, we had reason to believe, especially knowing the iron-willed patient as we did, that Mom's condition would improve, not deteriorate, from this point forward. At least it would improve before it deteriorated, which of course we knew it would do eventually. While I welcomed the prospect of having hospice involved with us, since it was obvious Dad and I, as primary caregivers, were going to need help, I, for one, did not want anyone, least of all my mother, to believe we had brought her home to die. We had brought her home to live! And I wanted to be sure that our hospice partners understood this from the get-go.

On the day following discharge from the hospital, Dad and I met with the hospice nurse who would be our case manager and lead partner while Claudia kept Mom company in the bedroom. We were asked many questions, including where we wanted to put the hospital bed that could be delivered within 24 hours. I didn't want a hospital bed. I didn't want it because I didn't think (was I entitled to an opinion on this?!) Mom really needed it yet; Claudia, Dad, and I all were capable of meeting her needs with the current arrangements, although we did think a big bed wedge (which was subsequently requisitioned for us) would help Mom sit more comfortably in her bed than if we were to prop pillows behind her. But the fact that we could handle things, or confidently assumed we could, was not the reason I gave Peggy for declining the hospital bed at this time.

I tearfully tried to explain to her that we had brought Mom home to live, not to die. While a hospital bed could be raised and lowered and make lots of things comfortable for patients and simpler for caregivers, a hospital bed also represents in very visible, tangible terms, let's be honest, a step closer to death. It is the place where a hospice patient *will* die. Moreover, were Mom to be in a hospital bed she would be in it alone, without her sweetheart. Hospital beds do not come in queen size! At this point in the conversation my father also spoke through tears. He made clear that it was very, very important to him that if Mom were to have pain or any issue in the night, or if she were to cry out for him, he wanted to be next to her so he could reach out and comfort her. They wanted—they needed—to sleep together. No hospital bed.

We did not want Mom to feel like a patient in her home; despite her increasing limitations and dependence on caregivers, she was still the lady of the house ... *her* house, the house where she *lived.*

Our hospice nurse understood, and she indulged our concerns and wishes with compassion and with gentle, caring touches. She was wonderful, and she reassured us that while hospice care anticipates death, hospice is as much about quality living as it is about comfortable, dignified dying. We were on the same page. We loved Peggy, from our first meeting to the hugs she gave each of us at Mom's celebration of life.

In the days that followed, Mom's left-side weakness did not improve; in fact, it had gotten worse. An evaluation by the hospice physical therapist on June 16 led him to recommend a hospital bed and a Hoyer lift so that transfers out of the bed and into a wheelchair or onto a commode could be done more easily and also safely. On his recommendation, the bed and lift were ordered; it seemed obvious to all on that particular morning that we needed it. My husband Joe and son Steve drove to Enfield from West Hartford in order to move the heavy furniture from the living room into the garage.

My father was visibly crushed; things were moving in the wrong direction. While Mom slept, the bed was set up in the living room, and the recliner chair was moved from the bedroom into the living room. We kept as much of the old furniture in place as we could so that the room still resembled what it had been previously. I purchased a bedspread that matched the furniture, and throw pillows that had been on the couches were tossed onto the hospital bed, making it look almost as though it belonged in that space.

We quickly resolved not to incorporate the term "hospital bed" into our vocabulary. From that day until the day Mom died in it, we referred to the hospital bed in her living room as her "day bed." She spent time in it during the day so that she could be part of the action in the main part of the house rather than isolated in her bedroom. The "day bed" was one of Mom's perches during the day, but it was *not* where she spent her nights. Until the final week of her life, Mom and Dad slept together in *their* bed, in their bedroom. And during her final week, Dad still slept next to her at night so that he could hear her, touch her, comfort her. He slept on an inflatable bed that nestled right up next to Mom's hospital bed, which was lowered at night so that it was at the same level as Dad's. Their eyes could meet. They could feel their breath on each other. He could smell the Chanel No. 5 he sprayed on her.

The Hoyer lift never made its way from the garage into the house. It was a monster, and I hated it despite its obvious advantages. Like the hospital bed, the lift sent a visual message that Mom's condition had deteriorated and was expected to continue on that path. We decided to hold off on its use (and not even mention it to Mom) until we were no longer able to help her help herself out of bed to use a walker (if she had sufficient leg strength) or climb into a wheelchair.

We had correctly predicted that Paula's presence could have greater value and impact if she delayed her next trip east until Mom was out of the hospital adjusting to her new condition and circumstances in the home environment. However, none of us predicted how well Mom would do, or how many (and how quickly) more good days and good times would follow. On June 17, less than twenty-four hours after the hospital bed had been delivered in response to what appeared to be a precipitous deterioration in Mom's condition (and prospects), I sent Eric and a few other folks some photos I'd taken earlier in the day, including a great picture of Mom and Dad that still hangs on Dad's fridge.

To everyone's surprise (not to mention utter delight), Mom had been strong enough to get out of bed, into the wheelchair, and out onto the deck to enjoy the beautiful afternoon. Eric was thrilled to read, and see in the photos, that, as he put it, "Mom was up, out, and about!"

From: Linda Campanella
Sent: Wednesday, June 17, 2009 5:48 PM
To: Eric Sachsse
Subject: RE: A beautiful day on the deck in Enfield!

She will be up, out, and about if I have anything to do about it. And I know you know what I mean by that (i.e., the spirit in which it is intended). I keep pushing for us to be in "living" mode rather than "dying" mode. I have urged that we not even show Mom the big lift that will move her from hospital bed to chair or commode or...It's bad enough that we have a hospital bed in the living room now—bad in terms of what it signals. But now we have options, and in truth I'm glad the bed is there.

I am more hopeful today than I was yesterday morning. I hope she has more living to do—*good* living. She is amazingly strong; that's all I can say...

But it's still an hour-by-hour deal. She could wake up from her nap and be terrible.

XO
LSC

There was indeed more good living to do. Plenty of it. Below, as an indication of some of the good times, are the dates and subject lines of e-mails I sent, with photos attached, to family and friends in the weeks that followed.

June 19:	Happy hour with neighbor Doris and friend Jim Polga
June 24:	Nan on deck!
July 1:	A special lunch guest (Bobye)
July 4:	July 4 gathering
July 11:	Morningside Visitors (Joan and Marty)
July 21:	Good times (Bev Gray's visit)
July 23:	Nan—Flower Child
July 23:	Out and About—At Outback!
July 24:	Today's Headband
July 28:	On our way to Stew Leonard's
August 1:	On the deck at Wildwood with Bobye
August 24:	Bev's visit
August 24:	Happy Hour 8/24
August 28:	Visit from the Woods

And this list is just a partial account of happy, sometimes magical, moments in the months following Mom's turn for the worse as a result of her major seizure May 31. When Dad went on August 4 to his annual check-up appointment with Dr. O'Neill, who had not seen Mom since he discharged her from the hospital and into hospice care on June 7, I sent him off with downloaded prints of a half dozen photos, each one with a caption providing the date. I was certain Dr. O'Neill would be absolutely thrilled, and perhaps also a bit shocked, to see how great Mom looked and how "active" she had been post-hospital. He had remained engaged in her care ever since her discharge, working in close partnership via telephone with our hospice nurse, but the photos vividly conveyed what no conversation could have impressed upon him: there was incredible joy in my mother's life and plenty of life left in my mother. She had gone home to live, not to die.

Doing

By early July, the house in Enfield was a busy place, with many comings and goings. At times it was dizzying. A hospice home health aide arrived each morning for what the three daughters euphemistically termed Mom's "spa treatment" (though it was hardly that). Initially we had five, at times six, different aides per week, each with a different name to remember and a unique personality to adjust to, and each coming at a slightly different hour of the morning. This really was too much for any of us to handle; we made clear to hospice that, as soon as possible, we wanted to reduce the number of aides to a handful who would all come at approximately the same time each day.

Mom was a great sport about the confusion these frequent, and frequently changing, visitors created. She always was genuinely delighted to greet a visitor, even if she had no memory of what her name was, which generally was the case. Impaired short-term recall was the only cognitive deficit we ever noticed in Mom throughout her ordeal—pretty amazing, given the crop of tumors that had sprouted in her brain. She laughed at herself when she called Anne "Robin," or said "Hello Sandy" to Michelle and told her how glad she was to see her again (on her first visit), or had no clue at all what Theresa's name was, though she recognized her infectious laugh. And the aides laughed with Mom, always and lovingly making it seem perfectly understandable (for reasons unrelated to cancer and dying) that Mom might get a little confused.

These aides truly were a special breed. So tender and yet so tough. Eventually we were able to consolidate the schedule so that fewer of them came. We understood without needing to be told that schedule adjustments were possible whenever another hospice patient passed away, thereby creating an opportunity for an aide who otherwise had been busy on a Thursday morning to be plugged into Mom's Thursday morning schedule. It didn't take too long before someone was available two mornings instead of just one. In hospice situations, patients pass away; that's just the business they are in. I cannot fathom how the women who cared for my mother—each one of whom treated Mom with respect, dignity, affection and tenderness, and each of whom entered a most intimate inner sanctum of our family's existence—found the strength to do what they do, day after day, family after family. So much anguish to observe, as patients and their families take the final steps toward death. So many sad goodbyes.

In addition to the home health aides who came every morning, hospice volunteers were plugged into our schedule for an hour-long visit with Mom two afternoons each week. Private health aides were hired to come several evenings a week so Dad would have another pair of hands and legs if Claudia or I were not there. We needed to keep a schedule on Dad's refrigerator to keep track of who-what-when.

From: Linda Campanella
Sent: Thursday, August 13, 2009 3:32 PM
To: Nan & Eck
Subject: schedule next week

Dad, as we agreed last week, *next week* (when Paula/all Blakers are here through Sunday 8/23, and when I will be in Essex) there will be *no hospice volunteers* (no Dolores on Wednesday and no Betty on Friday) and there will be *no Caring Solutions aides in the evenings.* (I took care of all the cancellations last week.) As usual, the *hospice aides will come at their regularly scheduled times each morning*, but Sandy will be on vacation and two different subs will be coming in her place (Claudia has their names).

If you decide to go away on day trips or for a few days running at Wildwood, the only canceling you'll need to do is with Home and Community (for the morning aides). You work on Monday 8/24. I plan to come to Enfield Sunday evening 8/23 and will stay overnight. I've also got you covered for the end of that week (you work Thursday and Friday).

Das ist Alles! Below is an updated schedule for your fridge reflecting the addition of Deborah (instead of Virginia) and reduced hours for the evening aides. This schedule will kick in again the week of August 23.

XO
LSC

	SUN.	MON.	TUES.	WED.	THUR.	FRI.	SAT.
Hospice aide	Anne 10:30	Robin 11:00	Sandy 10:45	Theresa 10:00	Sandy 10:45	Theresa 11:00	Anne 10:30
Volunteer				Dolores 1:30 – 2:30ish		Betty 1:30 – 2:30ish	
Private aide			Beverly 6:00 – 8:00	Beverly 6:00 – 8:00	Beverly 6:00 – 8:00	Deborah 6:00 – 8:00	Deborah 6:00 – 8:00

Some differences of perspective within the family relative to the "need" for hospice volunteers and evening aides created brief moments of tension, but the tension dissipated following honest exchanges with each other that clarified points of view.

Wed., August 12

Halloooo, Dad. As Claudia will tell/has told you, I was surprised and also disappointed to learn that Dolores' scheduled visit today was cancelled. Please allow me to explain why, in the hope you'll be open to and understand my perspective. I believe Claudia (who, by the way, had not yet personally observed Mom interacting with any hospice volunteers or evening aides) found it helpful to talk it through on the phone earlier, so that we are all on the same page more or less, or at least aware of and sensitive to each other's feelings.

When you told me you and Claudia wanted to cancel the evening aides for this week, I explained to you that what Beverly and Deborah do and provide (for/to Mom) goes way beyond what you, Claudia, and I are perfectly capable of doing. As you point out, we do not *need* them. However, Mom really *likes* being with them—even if she rolls her eyes and says she doesn't need any aides, and even if she can't remember any of their names or what they might have talked about an hour earlier…They bring *companionship*. They bring *interactions*. They bring *smiles* to Mom's face. They offer *empathy*. They provide an opportunity to talk about things she may not talk (and in some cases has not talked) with us/family about. They break up a deadly (pun *intended*) dull routine at home that, without the injection of distractions and human interactions associated with visitors, consists essentially of taking meds, eating meals, sitting on the commode, being washed, taking naps, and going out on the porch when she can. Thank you for agreeing to keep Beverly and Deborah in the picture this week for reasons that seemed to make sense to you at the time.

Mom also *loves* being with Dolores. Whenever a hospice volunteer (Dolores, Betty, or Faith) arrives, I go in another room and let their wonderful conversation flow privately, but I often overhear what is being said. It is *wonderful*. These people open up a whole new world for Mom. She and I talked about this just this past weekend and she absolutely,

Linda Campanella

strongly agreed that she enjoys these visits for that very reason. She knows my life, your life, Claudia's life inside and out; but these new friends—and they have become *friends*—have interesting backgrounds, challenges, pains, heartaches, perspectives, etc. that are new to Mom and allow her to explore new territory that injects newness and interest and life into her day. No, we caregivers do not *need* to take a break for an hour on Wednesdays and Fridays; nor does Mom *need* a visit from "a hospice volunteer." But Mom sure has enjoyed each and every visit by Dolores, Betty, and Faith. She has raved about Dolores, who is just fabulous with (and in my view *for*) Mom, and she couldn't stop talking about her visit (now visits) with Faith. She adores Beverly (and laughs constantly with her), and she immediately felt a connection with Deborah, whose caring touch and empathy were immediately felt and appreciated. As I mentioned to you, happy hour with Beverly—even if Beverly isn't *doing* anything (like hands-on care for Mom)—is providing a terrific service to *Mom* (as opposed to relief or help to us/caregivers). Let's keep welcoming the visits from people who have become new friends and now inject *interest* and something *to do* into her life.

This may sound like I am being critical or lecturing, and I truly, truly, truly am doing neither. I am trying hard to say things in a way that will not make you infer that I am upset or critical (as I have no right to be either!). When I spoke with Claudia, I told her I was disappointed that the visit from Dolores didn't happen today but *not* disappointed in *anyone*, her or you. Lord knows everyone is doing the best he/she can and what he/she thinks is best.

We were such a close family all along that it was a little shocking, and a lot discomfiting, whenever even a little tension entered the dynamic. Even close families will be tested in times like we were living through. Times like these, when a loved one is dying (and everyone else in the family is facing a dreaded loss), demand courage and patience for open, honest conversation to defuse tensions that might otherwise fester and erupt. When people with different DNA are involved in any situation, but perhaps especially when emotions are frayed to begin with and so much seems to be at stake, differences of opinion and different approaches to caring, loving, and even grieving are a given.

The key for us, I believe, was the ability to quickly see past whatever had crept to the surface to create division and refocus on what, beneath the surface, united us in common purpose. We understood that beneath whatever difference momentarily created misunderstanding or conflict was a shared desire to do the best each of us could and ultimately what was best overall for Mom. There is no right or wrong way—and no better or best way—to love someone. Occasionally we needed to stop and remind ourselves of this and validate each other in our unique personalities and approaches. The very last thing my mother ever, ever would have wanted was that her situation would cause friction or rifts in her family. This would have broken her heart, and we knew it.

When I wrote the e-mail to my father about how Mom's shrinking world opened up when she was visited by aides and volunteers, one of the key messages I sought to convey was the importance (at least from my perspective) of allowing Mom to make meaningful human connections through which she could be and share herself—as *Mensch*, not cancer patient. Though disease ate away at other organs, her heart was healthy, physically and figuratively; it remained a flowing font of empathy and other emotions that continued to pump powerfully through her veins, rendering her as beautifully human as she ever had been.

She was profoundly affected by the stories private aide Beverly shared when Mom inquired about her family. She learned, for example, that for nineteen years Beverly had been lovingly caring (to an extent almost unimaginable) for a granddaughter afflicted with a rare and especially debilitating variation of muscular dystrophy. Beverly spoke of her granddaughter, who could not swallow or talk or walk but was nevertheless a happy high school student, with such obvious pride and joy. Mom asked her to bring family photos to share, and one evening during happy hour they talked about their grandchildren, about pain, about joy, about courage. Mom listened, she shared, and she cared.

She was moved to tears by the story aide Deborah told about having cared for her quadriplegic husband, injured in a freak fall, for over ten years until his death at age fifty. A widow now, Deborah said with a smile that she would not have missed or traded a single day of their precious time together during those years. She recalled that her husband woke up every morning feeling happy to be alive. Mom listened, she shared, and she cared.

These stories—other people's stories, their joys and their sorrows—opened Mom's world beyond the boundaries imposed by her physical limitations. They tapped into a loving spirit that knew no boundaries or limitations. This was so good for her. She felt very alive during these moments of unbridled sharing and caring. They were moments in which she was giving, not just receiving.

My inclination to encourage such opportunities for interaction with non-family members also reflected my belief that it was important to continue finding or creating ways for my mother to realize she was still able "to do"—and that in fact she was still doing. Sharing and caring was *doing*. And there was more she could still do that would make her feel she was living. I tried to explain my feelings about the importance of doing in the second half of my message to Dad.

> …Speaking of *doing*…In my view, and I have on occasion tried to express this too, one of the best things any of us can do for Mom is to make her feel her life does *not* consist solely or mostly of having us do things *for* (and *to*) her. And we can do this by allowing and encouraging her to do things she either likes doing or *used to do* as a matter of routine life and would love to still do (if she could/can). She is most depressed when

she thinks about what she no longer does or can do and when she thinks about how totally dependent she has become.

On Friday night, she announced that she was "going to do laundry tomorrow"; well, I was sure going to find a way to make that happen, because to begin with I thought it was fantastic that she even had that thought! I have been hell-bent on injecting living into her dying—by encouraging her to *do* things and by reminding her of all the things she still *can* do (even if she can't do them well anymore)—from crossword puzzles to folding laundry to putting the silverware away when one of us empties the dishwasher to feeding herself to watering her plants (if I lift them down from the sill) to washing her own face to preparing a Hamburger Helper meal with me and key lime pie dessert with Beverly the other night to picking out your clothes to helping me with laundry to using toilet paper *herself* to grocery shopping at Stew Leonard's to going to the refrigerator to take out her own breakfast/yogurt to going out to a restaurant for dinner to getting up on the porch at Wildwood to...

"There's no need" or "It's my job" are things we all should probably avoid saying while we instead look for and find ways to encourage Mom to feel she is living, not dying; that she can still *do* rather than be done *to* or *for*. It can be a little taxing, and it can be a *lot* depressing if we let it be; trust me, I could have become very sad had I thought too long about the "help" I got from Mom in the laundry room. But while I noticed how little she could do, *she* felt like she had just helped me do a load of laundry. *That* made me feel great–for her.

As you would say, *end of speech*. I hope, hope, hope, hope you take all this in the spirit in which it is offered. I know how difficult all of this is for you (and, unfortunately, how awful it is yet to become). Far more difficult and painful than you let on (or than your children publicly acknowledge we understand—but we *do*). Your tenderness toward Mom and your care for her are both heartwarming and heartbreaking to observe. I realized a week or two ago that in my own eagerness to help/unburden you by doing for Mom while I am in Enfield, I might in some ways, but unknowingly/unintentionally, be in the way by being "in between"—limiting or diminishing you in a role you want and need to play with your sweetie; maybe I wasn't allowing you to receive Mom's "gift of giving" as fully as *you* might want. I adjusted my head a little (pulling back and giving you space in what is after all your own space, if you will). And I am truly sorry for any stepping on your toes I may have done.

Ewig,
Die Aelteste

Dad did receive this message in the spirit in which it was intended. I had seen ample evidence by then of his being open to input and ideas, as well as being a good source of them himself. In the weeks that followed, Mom did do more doing. And all of us—Dad, my siblings, and I—worked hard to respect and support each other as much as we sought to respect and support Mom. What *we* were doing was hard to do. It really was. And we needed each other.

In July I had shared with Dad some additional thoughts or suggestions regarding doing, dignity, and independence; that e-mail prompted Eric to suggest I might write a book, entitled "Living while Dying," to help guide others through the trials and trauma we were experiencing. Clearly he, at least, thought I was suggesting something potentially valuable.

From: Linda Campanella
Sent: Saturday, July 18, 2009 2:00 PM
To: Nan & Eck
Subject: THINGS TO THINK OF/REMEMBER

THINGS TO THINK ABOUT OR REMEMBER WHEN YOU ARE ALONE WITH NAN

Dad,
We want to encourage Mom in every way to know and feel that she is living, not dying. To exist in a hospital bed all

day long, even when there is interaction with others, doesn't feel much like living. The more she can get out of the bed, the better. The more *independent* she can feel, the less she will feel like either an invalid or an infant (totally helpless and dependent—and thus a burden). The more she can participate, even to a limited degree, in "regular" activities that feel like her "old life," the better; she will feel like she is *doing* something.

- When she is awake, she should wear her glasses.

- Wearing clothes during the day rather than a nightie/bathrobe makes a difference!

- She should have breakfast at the table; the sitting position should help initiate a bowel movement. She experiences more independence and, importantly, more dignity (not to mention comfort) using the commode.

- Offer the commode at various times in the day; even if she is unsuccessful, she will have exercised a bit to get onto the commode. Plus, she will have been given an option and allowed to make a decision.

- She should feed herself whenever possible; she can do it (albeit with assistance at certain moments). Being fed makes one feel like an infant, or just helpless.

- It might be good to encourage her to walk from bed to recliner once a day. Good exercise. Good independence.

- On days when there is no volunteer here from 1:30 to 3:30, perhaps she could invite one of her Autumn Fields neighbors for a quick visit while she is in the recliner. She loves the company and being connected to her friends/prior way of living. (Obviously, she won't always feel up to this, but on good days it might be a good idea.)

- Mom has not read a paper in weeks and weeks. A nice way to interact with her is to read to her from the newspaper so she feels connected/reconnected to the world. Even the obit page interests her.

LINDA CAMPANELLA

- Print e-mails that are of interest to her and read them; she doesn't get to the computer anymore, but people continue to send messages.

- Why not get back into the routine of watching the evening news together? No reason for her not to go into the TV room, whether for the news or a Red Sox game or...

- Music in the background is always nice. Listening to music while in bed is actually doing something; it's better than just lying there doing nothing, alone.

- Do the crossword puzzle in the living room and occasionally ask her to solve a clue.

- She could help fold washcloths and towels sitting at the dining room table.

- Close the curtains at the dining room table in the evening/at night. Since there is bathing and changing going on, we want to protect Mom's privacy.

With love,
LSC
7–18–09

In rereading that e-mail now, I am reminded of the indignities Mom suffered through without ever letting us believe she was suffering at all. There are no words to describe her courage or my awe. No one should have to go through what she went through, and yet I know so many do. The story of my mother's grace and courage could be told by daughters and sons across the globe, I'm sure.

In rereading it, I also am reminded of how receptive my father was to input. He was as open as he was, I believe, because he loved Mom so indescribably much that he would do or try just about anything to make her happy or comfortable. Remembering this makes me remember how much I also love him. No one should have to go through what *he* went through either.

Believing

The miracle

Within an hour of receiving the call from my father telling me of my mother's diagnosis, I sent an e-mail to Gary Miller, senior minister at Asylum Hill Congregational Church in Hartford. I told him the news and asked him to say a prayer for my mother, and also for my father. Then I added, "I've never pleaded with God for anything before, but I am about to begin a serious, selfish conversation." Gary reassured me that I was not alone and that, "late in the evening and first thing in the morning," my family would be held in prayer. "Let your inner light be a source of your strength and a partner in your tears," he encouraged me. I responded immediately.

From: Linda Campanella
Sent: Tuesday, September 09, 2008 7:12 AM
To: Gary Miller
Subject: RE: prayer

Thanks. I just hope my spirit can assist her in her journey and my father, who will be so lost without her. I am already suspecting that I see God at work in strange ways. Two weeks ago I resigned from the TheaterWorks board. My children are out of the "nest" as of two weeks ago. Did my mother's diagnosis mysteriously wait for a time when I will have time to take care of her and be a shoulder for my father to lean on, and cry on? … At least that's one of the thoughts I had during a sleepless night. Again, thank you for everything.

I have never been good at, or comfortable, praying. For one thing, my notion of God makes it difficult for me to pray *to* God, as though he/she/it were listening. I've also had a hard time shaking my sense that prayer is too often a selfish act that one resorts to, perhaps reflexively, when in need of something—mercy, forgiveness, health, wealth, love. This idea of asking for something has seemed in tension with my concept of Christianity or faith or religion as fundamentally unselfish; as a mechanism for giving, not taking. My thinking about this changed during the last year of my mother's life, and it changed significantly.

On January 27, she had a follow-up MRI of the brain because she had been experiencing more frequent headaches and related symptoms. My family was fearful of what the scans might reveal, while at the same time we were hopeful they might reveal unexpected good news. The results were better than we had dared hope for. Two of the tumors were no longer visible on the MRI. The third had shrunk to the point it was barely visible. The fourth—which was the largest one initially—also had shrunk measurably. There were no *new* growths. This was almost unbelievable! Too good to be true. We knew there was no cure for my mother's cancer, so this was no miracle; but the MRI result signaled that she would likely enjoy a reasonably good quality of life for a longer period of time than we had expected.

Could prayer have played a role in this?

When my head hit the pillow the night of January 27, I could not help but think about the many people, some whom I know and others I've never met, who had been holding my mother in their prayers. Many parishioners at Asylum Hill Congregational Church had told me over the preceding weeks and months that they were praying for my mother. My mother's cousin Ruthie's prayer group at Lakewood Baptist Church in Appomatox, Virginia, had been praying for her constantly; every week my mother received a card signed by each member of the group.

It was extraordinary to be falling asleep with positive thoughts about my mother's illness; too many nights I had cried myself to sleep, overwhelmed by my sadness. And I understood in that moment that prayer need not be and indeed *is not* a selfish act. All the wonderful people who prayed for my mother were giving, not taking, through prayer. And their generous gifts of love, delivered through prayer, may in some unknown and unknowable way have played a role in the good news my family received on January 27. What an awesome possibility!

My faith is about believing in what I cannot see, what I cannot explain, but what my heart tells me is possible. I believe that God is love, that God is good. I believe that this goodness—God's spirit, if you will—burns in each of us, reflecting and igniting our human potential to *do good*.

Suddenly, as I lay in bed January 27, I realized I was silently repeating the word "grateful" in my head, over and again ... *grateful ... grateful.* Then it occurred to me that I might actually be praying in that moment—a prayer of thankfulness. I went on to think about all the things in my life for which I am grateful. And in that moment I resolved to try to remember to pause *every* night as my head hits the pillow to reflect on the many blessings in my life and to be thankful for all that is good. If *God is good* (as I was taught in Sunday school to believe), then in being thankful for all that is good, I was thankful for God—whatever, whoever, wherever it is.

Over the years, Mom and I enjoyed contemplating, reading about, and discussing that very question: Who, what, where is God? At the end of July, by which time Mom was spending most of her days in the hospital bed situated in her living room, I read a book review in the *Hartford Courant* that caught my eye. It was a review of Connecticut College Professor Andrew Pessin's book *The God Question: What Famous Thinkers from Plato to Dawkins Have Said about the Divine.* I cut out the review and brought it with me on my next visit to Enfield, as there is a Barnes & Noble on the main drag in Enfield en route to my parents' house.

The book was perfect—not from a critic's perspective but in terms of my hope that it might be something I could read to Mom. It is a collection of ninety, two- or three-page essays, each of them engaging and easily accessible to the layperson, and each one illuminating a great thinker's view, yea or nay, on the question of God's existence. Although her body was not functioning particularly well anymore, Mom's mind was still sharp. Despite now having at least eleven cancerous growths in her brain, my mother remained, until the very end, the same curious, thoughtful, intellectually engaged, witty, gracious, loving person she always had been.

When she was first diagnosed, she was so afraid—and I don't think "afraid" is too strong a word—that growing lesions in her brain would cause her to lose her ability to laugh, to feel and express emotions, to give and receive love. I believe she feared this more than she feared death itself or any physical pain she might experience. My mother was herself, the person we had known and loved, until the very end of August, when she slipped into the comatose state that preceded her death. She never lost her sense of humor or her ability to feel and express love. Perhaps, if she ever prayed, she had asked God for that mercy. Perhaps God answered her prayer. It is possible.

I never expected a miracle. I didn't even pray for one. But I believe something miraculous happened as we traveled with Mom through the last year of her life knowing death was coming soon. To me, it was nothing short of a miracle that my mother remained so strong, so positive, so happy, and so thankful. As I wrote in July to her friend Kathy, I do not think it is possible to be as strong as my mother was without help from above … or somewhere!

From: Linda Campanella
Sent: Thursday, July 09, 2009 3:39 PM
To: Stu & Kathy Lohr
Subject: Nan

Dear Kathy,

There have been many wonderful family gatherings since her diagnosis last September; this family closeness is part of the silver lining in the cloud. We've managed to find and create so much joy these past ten months, believe it or not. And right at the center of all of it is an amazing woman who loves life and has exhibited more courage and strength than any of us could have imagined possible.

She has not given up the fight, despite some pretty tough times and lousy days. She said to the hospice spiritual counselor today, whom she was meeting for the first time, that she goes to sleep each night with a feeling of gratitude. She also said that she doesn't know how much longer she has but that she believes anything is possible, even miracles.

I believe the miracle in all this is not that she is still living or that she may live quite a while still, but rather that she has remained to strong, so positive, so joyful despite the death sentence she received last September—a time when she was feeling in the prime of her later years and looking forward to so much more wonderful living. I don't know how it is humanly possible not to despair or wallow in self-pity; she has done neither, and to me this *is* a miracle. Or God's grace.

My mother's strength has given her family strength. She continues to give us gifts each day. What a lady! And what a tough cookie!

So that's the story. Each day is still filled with a sparkle of joy. Sometimes the sparkle is actually a glow that lasts quite a while; we love those times! Beneath the smiles, though, we all have hearts that are breaking—none more so than my father's. The long goodbye has given us all opportunities we are grateful for, but it is so, so difficult to know someone you love to the core of your being is going to die—and to then watch the dying process, helpless to stop or reverse it. We are fortunate and thankful to have hospice walking this path with us; everyone we have encountered is both competent and compassionate, and this is indeed a special combination.

I know Mom will enjoy speaking with you again soon. Thank you for being such a faithful, caring friend. She has said countless times how much she cherishes these friendships and how both family *and friends* have been so wonderful to her. It is true!

Best,
Linda

The gift of giving

I think when any of us imagines ourselves gravely ill or dying, one of the things we fear most is being a burden to those we love most. My mother certainly seemed more distressed about how her situation was affecting her loved ones, especially as she became more dependent on us for her care, than she was about her own loss of independence and, eventually, dignity. While she was thankful beyond her ability to express appreciation, she was equally distressed that her husband and children were making sacrifices in their own lives in order to help her live what was left of hers.

From: Linda Campanella
Sent: Monday, January 19, 2009 10:24 AM
To: Nan & Eck
Subject: yesterday—and tomorrows

Dearest Mom,

Yesterday you said you were feeling "humiliated and ashamed." This statement has stuck with me—and gnawed at me. Please, please don't feel that way, especially not ashamed. Of what? You said you sleep the day away. So what? You said your family is making sacrifices. We (and that includes your in-law children) are not. We are doing what we *want* to do.

In some ways, your cancer is a gift to us. I, for one, see it as the gift of an opportunity to return the deep, unconditional love you have shown me for 51 years; an opportunity to make you realize, and feel, how much you mean to the people you've loved and taken care of all these years. You have never put yourself first. Let your children and your husband love you and take care of you the way you have done for us... and the way you would do if one of us were in your shoes. We will keep doing what we can do to help you through this ordeal.

Your cancer is a gift in another way. I consider every visit with you (and Dad), whether for an hour or a day, to be a gift. As I was nearly drowning in the initial grief I experienced over your diagnosis, people who'd walked in these shoes before me told me it could and probably would be a special time. I now understand what they were saying.

Every day, or every hour, that you are with us, and pain-free, is a day or hour we will cherish. I really enjoyed another "happy hour"—wine, a fire, Andrea Boccelli arias, some laughs—with you and Dad yesterday. Wouldn't trade it for anything. Life is good. I'm so glad, and so lucky, you are in my life.

At the same time, I have such admiration for you, for the will and courage you are showing. You are so strong! That said, I can only imagine how much strength (both physical and mental) it takes to get out of bed knowing what your day will be like; perhaps you have "no oomph" because it's all been consumed by the time you commit to a new day! But I do believe that even if you sleep for half or three-quarters of the day, if the day includes an hour such as we had by the fire last night, it's been a pretty good day. And there will be more good days, even if measured in hours, to come. The New Jersey trip, for example...

Please know that those who love you most and who will miss you more than you can possibly imagine consider you to be a gift, even in your current state. It would of course be great, *for you*, if you felt better and had more oomph; but it doesn't matter *to us* if you sleep most of the day away or need help in the bathroom or... We are so grateful you are here, with us. Let us do whatever we can to offer company, comfort, laughter, and whatever else you may need, now and later.

Don't feel sorry for us. Don't be ashamed . . . ever. Don't feel you have to be strong for us. And don't be afraid. Everything will be all right.

Love always,

Poo

On the very few occasions during her illness when she became noticeably, and ever so briefly, sad, her sadness was not about her own plight and prospects. I truly believe that, from the moment of her diagnosis to the moment she disappeared into a comatose state almost a year later, the anguish associated with causing her family to suffer emotionally was more painful to her than anything else.

She desperately did not want us to be sad; in fact, what I consider to have been her dying wish, expressed in one of the last conversations she had with my father, was articulated in three simple words: *Don't be sad.*

One of the most important moments in our experience came when my mother was largely homebound and bed-ridden in the hospital bed set up in her living room. This moment was important because of the immediate and enduring relief it provided my mother. The relief did not come in the form of medicine or any treatment of her body. The relief came in the form of comfort for the soul, and it was administered not by a physician or family member but by the spiritual counselor, aptly named Faith, who was a member of our hospice team.

Faith didn't visit often, but what happened on her first visit secured her a spot in my heart and ensured she would be asked to return for a future visit or visits. In keeping with my commitment to focus on living as opposed to dying, I was reluctant to engage the hospice spiritual counselor whose mission, as it had been explained to me, was largely to help a patient feel at peace about dying. (Dying? But we are still living!) Even as it was increasingly clear that my mother was getting closer to the end of her adventure with cancer, I continued to resist anything that might put a pall over her existence and remind her too suddenly or starkly how the story would end. Of course, we knew how it would end; but the story wasn't over yet.

However, I also believed it possible that my mother might feel inclined to share things with a spiritual counselor—especially one as gentle, kind, and intelligent as Faith appeared to be, based on a phone conversation I had had with her—that she would not want to share with family members. Fears, for example; maybe she would allow herself to be weak in the presence of someone for whom she did not feel it necessary to be strong.

I purposely scheduled Faith's visit on a day when my father, a self-proclaimed agnostic-verging-on-atheist, was at work. After the introductions, I disappeared into an adjoining room but was repeatedly called by my mother to join the conversation. She guessed, and was right, that I would be interested. Our shared interest in religion, our similar beliefs about God, our tendency to describe ourselves as "spiritual" as opposed to "religious" are among the many things that connected my mother and me so closely. She knew I would love to be part of her conversation with Faith and she welcomed me into this most intimate space.

Before I joined them, they spoke at some length about how each of them experienced God. My mother was very interested, and a little tickled, to learn that Faith, who studied world religions as an undergraduate and went on much later in life to earn a master's in divinity from Harvard, shared her unscholarly, somewhat unsophisticated belief that God is love. They also talked about having experienced what Faith called "Oh-wow moments" (often connected with nature) that ignite awareness of an awesome power or spirit mysteriously at work in our lives; these were moments that served to nurture and deepen their sense of spirituality.

Faith asked Mom how she was feeling or how she was doing and, in characteristic form, Mom did not focus on herself but instead deflected the focus of attention away from herself and onto others.

She admitted to feeling bad about the burden she felt she had become for her family. Faith quickly, and masterfully, disabused my mother of the notion, the painful misperception, that she was a burden to those who loved her. She acknowledged how difficult it must be for someone like Mom, who has been independent and in charge, someone who has been a nurturing, giving, loving mother and wife, to find herself out of control and in the position of needing to be cared for. She also deftly guided my mother to acknowledge how good it felt whenever *she* had had an opportunity to care for or help someone else over the course of her life. They agreed: Giving feels good.

Faith then opined that, in spending time with Mom and caring for her, family members were doing something we wanted to do; we were choosing to be with her, to take care of her, to spend time away from our spouses and homes, to make it possible for her to stay at home herself. Faith further suggested—and I quickly affirmed—that we all felt good, not bad or burdened, because we were in a position to return some of the unending, unconditional love she had given to all of us throughout our lifetimes. Mom had guided and nursed her four children into life, and now, in a similar sort of form-altering transition, we would guide and nurse Mom into death, "birthing" her into whatever comes next. Though it was difficult for me to converse with Mom about her death in such a direct way, primarily because I feared it would be difficult or dispiriting for *her*, both she and I seemed to find comfort and purpose in Faith's life-affirming message.

Then Faith told my mother something that completely changed the way she thought about her own situation and in turn ours. She said to Mom, "You have given them the gift of giving." Rather than being a burden to her family, Faith explained, the caring for her in her illness represented a *gift* to us—a gift from her. She was allowing us to help her, to give back, to love unconditionally. Viewing her plight through this prism made it possible, and more importantly made it logical and okay, to believe she was not a burden to her loved ones. In that ah-ha moment with Faith, my mother's heart was no longer as heavy as it had been. I could see the relief in her face.

The only one who had been feeling burdened was my mother; she had been suffering under the fear that she was, as she put it, "causing such a commotion" for all of us and disrupting our lives. In accepting that she was giving us a precious gift rather than extracting a heavy toll, my mother became unburdened. That unburdening, in itself, felt like a gift to us—one of the many reasons my family feels indebted to our hospice team. Mom knew then that although the prospect of losing her made us unspeakably sad, we were eternally grateful that her dying presented us the opportunity to wrap her tightly in our undying love.

She shed the final vestiges of the terrible burden she had been carrying—the burden of believing one is a burden—as she relayed the story of Faith's visit and message to my father that evening when he came home from work, to my sister Paula in Washington during a phone conversation that was the longest, most lucid and animated conversation Mom had had with anyone in days, and later to her dear friend Bobye. Each time she told someone what Faith had told her, I could see that she was more relieved and believed even more deeply that we had received, and would always cherish, her gift of giving.

LINDA CAMPANELLA

a beginning, not an end

When Mom was first diagnosed and I was an emotional wreck, friends who had traveled this path before told me with great confidence that, although I might not be able to understand or believe it yet, what lay ahead for me would in many ways be beautiful; they promised that the worst of times could be the best of times. Some of them said that their parent's death had been the most intensely spiritual experience of their lives.

My mother's death was both an intense and a spiritual experience for me. It wasn't "intensely spiritual," but there was a decidedly spiritual dimension to it, a dimension that I found helpful, especially in the days and weeks after Mom died. In her first conversation with my mother, Faith, the hospice spiritual counselor, spoke of death (even though it was not the subject I particularly wanted her to focus on!) as a beginning rather than an end. There is nothing new or terribly profound about that statement, except perhaps when one finds oneself confronting death, either one's own or the death of a loved one. It is in these moments when one desperately wants to believe that not everything dies or ends when the last breath is taken.

Those who will be left behind want to believe that we can and will remain connected to those whose physical presence we no longer experience. When we lose someone, we also want to believe that those we miss know how much they are missed and how much they were, and still are, loved; we want to believe they know when we are thinking of them, that they can still feel or sense our love. We look for signs of their abiding love and presence in our lives.

Without ever proselytizing, which is one reason we welcomed her into our most intimate thoughts and time in our lives, Faith shared her belief that, while we cannot know what comes after death, there is no reason *not* to believe that something–an unknown state or experience–begins when life as we know it ends. She spoke of the near-death experiences chronicled by Dr. Elisabeth Kübler Ross, psychiatrist, humanitarian, author, and pioneer of bereavement and hospice care; and she shared some stories told by dying people she herself had encountered. These, Faith suggested, provide sufficient grounds to believe at least in the *possibility* of something new, a new beginning.

She also suggested it might be helpful to think of death as one more major change in the cycle of life, just as getting married, moving to a new location, switching careers, starting a family represent unsettling transitions. Before we make any of these big changes in our lives, she explained, we feel anxious, because we are uncertain what our lives will be like afterwards; we are anxious about what is unknown. Death certainly changes everything, and the only *known* thing about death is that life on earth as we have experienced it ends. The rest is unknown … and unknowable. Faith encouraged us to think of death not as an end but as a change—a transition to something new, something unknown, something that may well prove to be even more wonderful than what has preceded it.

My mother and I had little trouble embracing the possibility that something wonderful may be on the other side of death and that the living and the dead remain connected after death in ways both can feel. I believe my father also embraced this possibility. He managed to embrace it despite being an agnostic and someone whose spiritual self was never evident to anyone in our family until my mother's diagnosis, at which time he began to reveal it, privately and in very subtle ways, to my mother. She knew Dad's grieving over the certainty she would lose her battle against death made him seek comfort in the possibility that, when she died, he would not altogether and forever lose her or what they were together. He also wanted to believe she would be at peace when her life ended. For these and perhaps other reasons, my father probably needed to believe Mom would be, or exist, "somewhere" else after she was gone.

As far as I could tell, Mom did believe this in her heart of hearts, and her faith bolstered mine. Months before her death she shared with me three favorite quotes that she hoped would be shared at her "celebration of life" gathering. Of these quotes, the one I chose to print first on her memorial card was this statement attributed to Saint John Chrysostom: "He whom you loved and lost is no longer where he was; he is now wherever you are."

Faith also helped Mom think of death itself as something beautiful, nothing to be feared. I recall that, during their first meeting, Faith had listened astutely enough to what my mother shared about her life and her faith that she intuitively chose to read the following poem to Mom, who closed her eyes while listening.

> Deep wet moss and cool blue shadows
> Beneath a bending fir,
> And the purple solitude of mountains,
> When only the dark owls stir—
> Oh, there will come a day, a twilight,
> When I shall sink to rest
> In deep wet moss and cool blue shadows
> Upon a mountain's breast,
> And yield a body torn with passions,
> And bruised with earthly scars,
> To the cool oblivion of evening,
> Of solitude and stars.

Mom was visibly moved and seemed reassured or comforted by the image suggested by these lines, written by Lew Sarett[1]. She told Faith she had loved the poem and its message. I believe she really did.

On Faith's third visit to the house, she and I were joined in conversation by my father and also one of my siblings for the first time. By this point, my mother was a week away from death and no longer communicating. As we finally accepted the inevitable as being now also imminent, our meeting with Faith was, for me, a profoundly moving meeting for reasons relating principally to what my father shared; I will expound on this in pages that follow. What I want to touch on here is that, although I didn't realize it at the time, this meeting foreshadowed the very difficult grieving experience one of us would have after Mom's death; although I observed it largely from a distance, clearly one sibling's grief was unlike what anyone else in the family experienced. As I thought about why this might be, I rather quickly came to the hypothesis that what distinguished it was quite possibly the fact that for this sibling, death is an end. Period, full stop.

---

1   Faith read this poem from a well-worn copy of *LIFE PRAYERS: From Around the World, 365 Prayers, Blessings, and Affirmations to Celebrate the Human Journey*, edited by Elizabeth Roberts and Elias Amidon (p. 329). It was, we learned, a book she brought with her on virtually all her visits with hospice patients in case there might be occasion to share something from it. On Nov. 19, 2009 I called Faith to ask her to remind me of the title of the poem she had read to Mom so that I could *Google* and find it on the Internet and then include it in what I was writing. She found it in her book and read it to me on the phone, wishing to confirm she and I were thinking of the same verse; the only clue I had been able to offer was that the word "moss" appeared prominently, and the poem, as I recalled it, offered a beautiful nature-focused metaphor for death. After she finished reading I told her, through the tears that started flowing almost as soon as she had started reading, that indeed she had found the right verse. After we hung up to end the conversation, I proceeded to order the book on amazon.com.

This point was made very clear in the meeting with Faith, when my sibling confessed to being unable to make the leap of faith necessary to believe in the possibility that Mom's spirit, her soul, would live on and be present in our lives in sometimes palpable, if mysterious, ways. The rest of us could make sense of Saint John Chrysostom's proposition: Mom would no longer be where she was; but she would always be wherever we were. She would "live" in our hearts, and we would remain connected in ways I could and would feel. All my sibling could think of when fast-forwarding was that that Mom would be dead. Not "living" anywhere. Gone. Forever.

The poem by Lew Sarett was read aloud one more time, the morning of September 9, 2009, as my family stood around Mom's bed holding hands, willing her to let go, to let her spirit soar on clouds of love. Sensing that her journey was ending, we had summoned our hospice nurse, and she in turn had summoned Faith. In that moment around Mom's bed we all were summoning faith, I suppose. I don't know if Mom heard the poem—hearing reportedly is the last sense one loses as our bodies shut down—but I hope she did. I hope she heard all the things each of us told her in those final days, hours, and moments.

In the days and weeks following Mom's death, Dad and three of his children managed not to be consumed or undone by our grief. We found comfort in, among other things, beliefs and possibilities nurtured by our individual spirituality. Each one of us believes different things; but all of us believe in God, or the possibility of God, and for us this belief allows us to think of and experience death differently than the sibling who seemed especially bereft. In mentioning this, I do not mean to suggest that any one of Mom's four children loved her more or less, or misses her more or less, than the others; nor do I mean to imply there is a right or wrong, better or worse way to grieve. There is only a personal way to grieve, a way that is different for everyone fundamentally and primarily because everyone's interconnectedness with a loved one who dies is unique.

I am thankful for the leaps of faith I was able to make, for these leaps took me to places of comfort following Mom's death, places I know not everyone is able to reach. For as long as I can remember I had been unable to grasp what people mean when they say they "found strength in their faith" or "called on their faith" to help them through times of terrible pain or challenge in their lives. I was simultaneously skeptical and awe-struck that someone's faith could provide so much support. My skepticism and awe probably resulted from two facts of my existence: I have not been a religious person and, until rather recently, not even a terribly spiritual person (or at least not particularly aware of my spirituality); and I have suffered no tragedy or crisis in my life that has tested my faith. The same could be said of my mother.

In July, at a time when she wasn't feeling particularly well and probably was imagining, yet again, that the end must be beginning, Mom did seem to reach out, in a very soft and subtle way, for spiritual nourishment that might bolster her faith. One day she asked me out of the blue, "What is his name? Is it Doug, or Gary, or ... ?"

"Who, Mom?" I asked in return. "Are you thinking of Gary Miller, my minister?"

"Yes," she said. It was Reverend Gary Miller, senior pastor at Asylum Hill Congregational Church in Hartford, whose name she had tried to recall. Although I suspected I knew why, I asked her why she had been thinking about Gary. She told me she had been thinking about dying and also about how good my church had been to her during the past year. It is true: She had been lifted in prayer many times by many people who knew from remarks I had shared during a worship service in October that my mother was terminally ill.

"I think I'd like to join Asylum Hill Church," she announced.

My parents had not belonged to a church in many years, and even when they belonged and supported First Church in Longmeadow, Massachusetts, they were not faithful attendees. Raised in the Episcopal church, my mother sometimes described herself as an agnostic; but in her heart she was a believer. Her straightforward spiritual lesson to her children was her belief that God is, simply put, love.

From: Nan & Eck
Sent: Sunday, September 14, 2008 4:37 AM
To: Linda Campanella
Subject: Fw:

Poo,

Below is some of what I just wrote to Clare. I feel like sharing. You are one of the few people I talk with about God so some of this may be of interest.

This time of night seems to have become my "witching hour!" And it also has become my e-mail hour for lack of many other things-to-do-choices. Problem is, my vision is not great so e-mails are full of typos ... I think you will forgive your grandmother.

Yes, my life has changed dramatically in just the past week! I do not want to be too "wordy," although there is certainly much I could say/write. Of course it is difficult to know that there is no cure and that it is just a matter of time, but it sure brings things into perspective! I am right now feeling very, very strong, able to be in the moment and take it one day at a time. Once I start therapy this may change; I have no idea how this will affect me. I do know, however, that I am the luckiest patient alive. Opa has arranged everything for me and has been in every single way just beyond belief wonderful. I am greatly blessed to have him. And I am blessed, so very, very blessed, to have my wonderful, wonderful family. My four children: amazing, every one. Ah, so lucky am I! And the greatest grandchildren in the world.

In this situation of mine, things are truly put into perspective. (I warn you, this is not going to be a well-written essay ... It will just pour out as is.) Love becomes indeed the operative word. I have so much of it! I have so much of it given to me, I have so much of it to give. You know, I think, that I am not very much an "organized religion" person. But I have a very deep faith. My belief is

totally basic. God is love. This simple belief seems to cover every-
thing I need to know or feel. All that is good and loving.... in me,
in you, in everyone, in the world is from God, is God in us. I think
you can understand my special belief.

Many things come into play here. Forgiveness is a very big
thing. Simply said, I do not want to die needing to forgive any-
one or needing to be forgiven by anyone. In this I am particularly
fortunate. No one has ever hurt me badly. I have no one I need to
forgive for anything. Just imagine that! What a charmed life I have
led! Also, I truly believe I have never caused anyone, ever, any real
pain ... and I am truly able to forgive myself my wrongdoings, Yes,
they have been many, but none, I think and believe, really serious.
It is a good feeling.

Over the last fifteen years, Mom had been to church with me at
Asylum Hill on quite a few occasions: the confirmations of my three
sons, a few Christmas Eve and Easter services, and several times in
between. Her sudden wish to join my church in July 2009 touched
me in several ways. It struck me as a poignant expression of her
unspoken questions, of a wish to be reassured of something, whatever it migh have been. Since being diagnosed, she had not acknowledged deep thoughts about death; nor had she revealed the almost
childlike vulnerability I sensed in that moment when she admitted
she might like to join Asylum Hill Church. For me, this reaching
out to be part of a faith community as the end of her life approached
was an important step. It reflected, in addition to whatever doubts
she might have, her quiet acceptance of reality, of her fate.

I told her I thought it was a great idea and that we should plan to
get back to Asylum Hill for a service when she was up to it. Sadly,
I never believed it would happen; I'm sure she didn't either, but we
both nodded in agreement that we would plan on it. I am very sorry
this return trip to my church, which loved her without even knowing
her, except through me, did not happen. There are so many things
that never happened again—and never will.

The next time I spoke with Gary—he and I spoke often, as I was serving as moderator of the church at the time—I mentioned my mother's comments, and he didn't hesitate a moment before saying Mom would be welcomed as a member and that a certificate of membership would be prepared that very day. Later that afternoon, his assistant e-mailed me to request the correct spelling of Mom's name, and within a few days the certificate, displaying *Nancy L. Sachsse* in beautiful calligraphy, was in my hands.

A week or so later, Mom was feeling well enough for me to suggest she and Dad make a trip to my home in West Hartford for *Kaffee und Kuchen*. To my delight, they thought she was up to it, and so they came. It would be the last time she came to my house. We had a lovely visit, sitting on the side porch sipping coffee and eating pastries carefully selected at Au Bon Pain by my husband, who recalled from a prior visit there with my folks which variety of goodies each of them loved best. While we were gathered and gabbing, I surprised Mom with the certificate of membership. None of us could hold back the tears. It was truly such a generous, wonderful gesture on the part of the church and its leaders, and I will always remain profoundly grateful because I saw how deeply moved she was.

The next time I visited her in Enfield we agreed that she should send a thank-you note to Gary. She asked me if I would take care of this for her, since she could no longer write, but I convinced her to tell me what she would like to say so that the message would be hers, not mine. She shared some thoughts and a few sentences with me, and I jotted them down. Later that evening, back home in West Hartford, I composed the note, building on what she had outlined. Since by now she also struggled to read (as a result of whatever the brain tumors were doing to her vision), I read the note aloud to her (and Dad) the next day as we ate dinner together in Enfield. This was the only time since her diagnosis—the *only* time—that I saw her sob. And just as suddenly as the crying began, it stopped.

I asked if she thought maybe she could sign her name. She struggled, but she did it. She wrote, "Very truly yours, Nancy," and these were the last words she ever wrote.

– 2 –

I have appreciated your prayers and prayers of members of the congregation these past months. Asylum Hill Church has been good to me and I am grateful. I am grateful for many things, and my last thought before I fall asleep each night is that I am so very thankful.

Very truly yours,
Nancy

Dear Rev. Miller,   8-10-09

Linda is writing my words as I speak them, as I am no longer able to write, but that cannot be an excuse for not conveying my heartfelt thanks. Your reaching out to offer me membership at Asylum Hill Church deeply touched me and gave me a wonderful, warm feeling to be included in such a caring group of people. It was one of the "wow moments" the hospice spiritual counselor and I talked about when talking about how we experience God. I do hope to get back to AHCC for a service soon. Over the years I have always felt at home there and understand why Linda loves this church so much.

Medicine for the heart and soul

Gary came to visit Mom on August 29. It was a pastoral call, to be sure, but we, and he, told her he had been in the area and just wanted to stop in and say hello to Asylum Hill Church's newest member. I had told him the family was sensing that she had begun making swifter progress toward the end of her journey, and he in turn had offered to pay my folks a visit.

Mom looked forward to his coming. And she looked lovely, sporting a colorful headband to match her blouse and donning the pair of earrings I especially liked to see her wear. She was seated in her recliner, not the hospital bed, when her guest arrived. When the doorbell rang I refreshed her lipstick and noticed her eyes were sparkling. There was a childlike anticipation on her face; she still loved visitors and long ago had stopped being concerned about what she looked like. I thought she was absolutely beautiful.

Apparently Gary did, too. He greeted her jovially and warmly, and he immediately admired her earrings, telling her she had picked an especially pretty pair. Their back-and-forth banter was so uplifting for us all. It was as though they were long-lost friends so happy to see each other again.

Dad had agreed to this visit on the condition that Gary "not give her last rites." He was making a point: He did not want the visit to feel funereal or the mood to be maudlin. Like me, Dad was uncomfortable talking about death in Mom's presence, or appearing in any way to prepare her for it, for fear of suggesting to her that we believed she was dying instead of living. We simply didn't want her to feel like she was dying, even though all of us, herself included, knew she had begun dying the day she was diagnosed.

Dad was nothing short of heroic in the encouragement he gave her for the entire duration of her yearlong battle. He willed her to live, and she wanted to live *for him*. To the end, he wanted and tried to protect her from whatever fear or distress the idea, or imminence, of death might spark in her.

I forewarned Gary, and he understood completely. He did eventually talk about death, but in an utterly appropriate and affirming way that gave Mom an opportunity to express her own thoughts, if she wanted to. She needed, and deserved, this opportunity. The importance of her being able to unload deep, gnawing thoughts became even more apparent when she spoke; it was obvious in what she shared. She told Gary, and also Dad and me, as we were part of the conversation, that while she was not afraid of dying, she was "afraid of missing my family." I can't write that without crying, because I know it to be true. Her family was her life; undoubtedly, she loved her family more than life itself. Wherever she was going next, she knew she could not bring her family with her, and she didn't want to be without us. Our hearts broke a little more in that moment of confession. Of course, we didn't want to be without her, either. And while she could not know for sure that she would miss us when she was no longer with us on earth, we were only too sure that, as those left behind, we would miss her every day for the rest of our lives.

Gary's response was lovely and loving, focusing on the relationship between my parents. He had observed immediately how deeply they adored each other, and he knew they had recently celebrated their fifty-second wedding anniversary. He also could quickly see the sorrow written on my father's face; despite wanting to be strong for my mother, in these intimate moments of sharing he could not hide his weakness.

Recalling what had comforted him after his mother died, Gary shared a line of scripture that he thought might be reassuring and comforting to both my parents as they confronted the heart-wrenching reality that Mom's death would separate them, causing them to miss each other terribly. Gary said, looking directly into their eyes in a way that suggested he was speaking with authority and conviction:

I leave you now and you have sorrow.
But I will see you again . . .
And, the next time . . .
Our joy will last forever.

He had paraphrased John 16:22:

You have sorrow now,
but I will see you again
and your heart will rejoice,
and no one will take your joy from you.

Through my tears, I could see they both wanted to believe these words to be true. Dad was crying, too. Mom was smiling. These words, if she believed them, had given her something to look forward to, I suppose.

More lighthearted conversation followed, and then Gary reached his hands out to us and asked if we would like to join him in a prayer before he left us to continue our day. To my surprise, my father quickly raised his hands and with one grabbed my right hand and with the other took hold of Mom's left hand. I had never prayed with my father. Prayer had not been part of our shared experience. To be honest, I wasn't even sure he would be open to participating.

When the four of us were connected in a circle, we bowed our heads and Gary spoke. I do not remember what exactly he said, but I recall very clearly how well he chose and spoke his message. When he was done, Dad and I lifted our heads, opened our tear-soaked eyes. Mom kept her head down and her eyes remained closed. She stayed still like that for quite a while, and eventually Dad said quietly to Gary, "She seems at peace." Then, choking up to the point he could no longer hold back the tears, he stood up and walked into the den.

Eventually Mom lifted her head and opened her eyes. She thanked Gary. He told her he would return in a few days, if she didn't mind, because he had thought of a book he would like to share with her. "Oh great, please do come back!" she replied. Then, with characteristic wit, she added, "I'll be sure to wear these earrings you like so much."

From: Linda Campanella
Sent: Sunday, August 30, 2009 8:43 AM
To: Gary Miller
Subject: Your Visit

Thank you again for your visit to Enfield yesterday, Gary. It meant a lot to me, and, more importantly, I believe your visit was deeply meaningful and helpful to *both* my parents. As my dad observed, Mom seemed so peaceful/at peace; this, above all perhaps, was good for my father to see. Following your prayer, she seemed most at peace. I found myself wishing at that moment that she would go to sleep forever. It's the first time I felt that way—ready to let go myself, believing that if she died in that moment she, and he, would know it was a good, beautiful thing...the continuation, not end, of a journey. After you left, she did fall asleep. I kept looking at her chest to see if she was still breathing, half-hoping she wasn't. These are, of course, thoughts that are difficult to explain or put into words, but I'm sure you understand. I share them with you only to impress upon you how lovely your visit was and how grateful my family is.

The other four Campanellas came to Enfield later in the day, essentially to say good-bye. Steve heads to Florence, Italy for a semester this afternoon, Phil goes back to college in Maine later in the week, and Paul will return to his apartment and job in Philadelphia. My boys have grown up with my parents and are extremely close to them. The good-bye was heart-wrenching for Steven (and so also for me). My mother was not herself in the afternoon. A vacant look had come over her, as the attached family photo shows, and conversation was difficult.

Your gentle, jolly, reassuring presence in the morning clearly was good medicine for her at the time. I'm sure its effects will be long-lasting, continuing to soothe her in the days ahead.

Thank you so much for everything.

Linda

During Gary's visit that Saturday morning, my mother had been interactive, happy, essentially a weak, tired version of herself. That afternoon, soon after he left, she disappeared into herself; her eyes took on a distant, empty look. On Sunday, she barely awoke and interacted very little. She clearly had begun to die. And it also was clear that I, and I believe also my father, had begun to accept in our hearts that it was time for Mom's body to succumb to the inevitable so that her beautiful spirit could be set free.

I will never fully understand, let alone be able to explain, the significance or impact of Gary's visit from my perspective. If ever there was an "intensely spiritual" moment of the sort predicted by friends, this was that moment. I trust even non-believers would have no trouble appreciating why I might have believed then, and still do today, that a divine and extraordinary power at work in our lives, call it God if you so incline, may have helped my minister from Asylum Hill Church in Hartford know that he would do important work in Enfield if he were to go soon; it had been Gary himself, not I, who decided on the prior Wednesday that it might be a good idea for him to pay a visit to my mother in the next few days. And perhaps even non-believers would also understand why I might believe that this unseen and unfathomable power at work in our lives, embodied on that Saturday in the person of a caring and compassionate minister, lovingly helped my mother begin letting go.

Doesn't it also make sense that it had been impossible for Mom to stop holding onto life and start embracing death as a beginning, the start of something unknown and potentially wondrous, until she could believe there was no reason to be afraid she would miss us, the family she loved more than life itself?

From that point on, until she took her very last breath, we continued to heap piles of love on my beautiful mother, reassuring her, and ourselves, that everything was and would be okay. Most importantly, we reassured her, even when we were no longer certain she could hear our whispers in her ear, that she would be taking us and our love with her wherever she was going next; that she would see us again, and "this time our joy will last forever."

LINDA CAMPANELLA

Letting go

No more tears

After Gary's departure, Dad returned to Mom's side and reassured her, since the subject of death and dying had been broached, that she should not "get the impression that you have begun to die. It's not time yet, sweetie pie. You're doing good."

My father, a native German who has lived in this country since 1956, speaks flawless English and surely would score 100 on any grammar quiz. Of course, he knew "doing good" was not grammatically correct. But he had adopted "You're doing good" as a phrase to encourage and reassure Mom and, no doubt, himself that all was okay; she was hanging in there; she was living, not dying. "Things are moving in the right direction," as my siblings will recall, was another signature line, especially in the weeks and months following Mom's major seizure and hospitalization in early June. These expressions endeared him to us. Even when she wasn't doing good (or well), he would encourage her to keep the faith. "Things are moving in the right direction, sweetie pie."

During her conversation with Gary, Mom had told him Dad made a solemn vow after her diagnosis. He promised her that no matter what they might encounter on the road ahead, he would never lie to her; she could count on him to be honest even when the truth was painful. I wasn't surprised by this, but it was a fact I hadn't known until that moment. In choosing to mention Dad's promise to Gary, and also in the way she spoke about it, she made obvious to all, including Dad, how enormously important and helpful this had been for her.

Dad was her Rock of Gibraltar. Her "knight in shining armor," as she said so often in the final weeks of her life. In the days following her diagnosis and not infrequently thereafter, she also called him her "hero." This title was generally conferred to convey how thankful she was that her husband was a highly respected and still practicing physician who could help her navigate the swelling sea of medical information; someone who, with her, would chart a decision course that made the most sense given the odds and options she was presented.

I can only imagine the enormous dual burden he bore as both husband and doctor. As a radiologist he needed (and wanted) to defer to colleagues in other fields and specialties when it came to Mom's treatment, but there was no one on earth she trusted more than her husband-hero. He wanted nothing more than to save her, though of course it was well beyond his (or anyone's) ability to do so; and if he couldn't save her life, he wanted to save her from any suffering.

Dad had tremendous respect for my mother's physicians, and, when hospice care began in June, he quickly developed an implicit trust in the superb nurse assigned to Mom. Despite this, I believe he put more pressure on himself, particularly in the final months of intensive home care, than he needed to. He was simultaneously afraid of losing her *and* of not making the best medical decisions about how to help her. In retrospect, it is clear he made, and thankfully believes he made, the best decisions, right decisions. But the road was rocky at times, and it extracted an incalculable toll.

As was inevitable, the day did eventually come when it was obvious to Dad that things were not "moving in the right direction" any longer. They were moving in the wrong direction. This happened in mid-August. Early in the month, we were still wishfully expecting a return to Wildwood for the visit of Paula and her family, starting

August 16, would be possible for Mom, but in view of her profound weakness and fatigue, that adventure proved not to be a viable option.

In the preceding months, Dad had on only a very few occasions cried in front of us; he would hasten to grab a tissue and move into a different room, alone and away from us. We allowed him space and privacy, respecting what a private (and, on the surface at least, unemotional) person he always has been. In August, when he had stopped saying or believing "things are moving in the right direction," the tears came more often. They often came while he was sitting next to Mom's bed watching her sleep and no doubt letting his mind wander to places that made him terribly sad.

In her final weeks, clearly sensing herself, even if only subconsciously, that things were no longer moving in the right direction, Mom began to say to Dad in German, *Bleib bei mir.* (Stay by me.) Increasingly she wanted him to stay by her side; she needed to feel his presence. Apparently, from hospice materials I had read, this reaction is common as the dying process progresses. My father was by her side as much as he could bear to be; he would get up when he needed a tissue to wipe his tears or blow his nose. The crying became very public (inside the house) and very regular.

She was dying, and so was a part of him. On numerous occasions during this final stretch, he would get up from her bedside and, with a tone of resignation or defeat that betrayed the depth of his anguish and pain, he would softly announce to whichever of his children was nearby, "I have no more tears."

But he was wrong. The tears kept coming. He cried rivers.

When my mother had taken the final turn toward the end and lay essentially lifeless in bed, my father did agree to have a conversation with Faith, the spiritual counselor from hospice. He had not wanted to meet with her previously, though he supported the idea of Mom's spending time with her "if it would be good for her." When he sat with Faith out on the back deck for conversation that afternoon, it wasn't much of a conversation. For the most part, he listened, often tearfully, to whatever she offered up in an effort to console and reassure us. He said little, but what he said was big. He shared something profound and profoundly moving, particularly since it was so personal and confessional coming from a man who was so private and, as he explained and later translated for Faith, *nüchtern*.

"I have learned how to cry," Dad said through his tears.

My father has never been one to show emotions or talk about feelings. His children always knew, beyond any doubt, how much he loved us, but we discerned this from what he did for us, not from what he said. As Faith was leaving that afternoon, Dad called her into the den, where he was grabbing his German-American dictionary off the bookshelf for her. He flipped through the Ns to *nüchtern*. Translation: aloof, rational, businesslike, unemotional. *Nüchtern* is a trait he believes was first recognized and labeled by his mother, and he characterized it as a "stigma since childhood."

He went on to explain to Faith (and also to me, as I was hearing this tale of *nüchtern* for the first time) that, as a young boy growing up in Nazi Germany under Hitler's regime, it had been deeply ingrained in him that, first of all, men should not cry and, above all, German men should never cry. And so he didn't. While many people think a man's crying represents strength, not weakness, clearly that philosophy did not prevail in Hitler's Germany and the schools my father attended.

It had taken a long time, but at last Dad was able express his feelings, his heartache. He was able to cry. He stopped fighting or hiding the impulse. To be honest, I'm not sure he had the strength anymore.

From: Christina Ripple
Sent: Tuesday, September 08, 2009 5:07 PM
To: Linda Campanella
Subject:

Please, please, please don't think that *any* request you make is a bother. I'm happy to ease your work-load however I can.

I feel so for you and your Dad. The only consolation I can give you is that, for you, the daughter, this is the worst time. Although there will be huge and unexpected grief when your Mom dies, you'll hopefully get some comfort from the fact that it's finally over and you gave her the greatest gift—a good death. Your father will be terribly lonely for a long time I'm sure. My dad was and actually came to our house for dinner almost every night for a good ten months! He, like your father, never cried before Mom died. He came from stoic Scottish descent and always hid his vulnerable side. When Mom was sick and after she died, he also wept often and easily and actually still does nine years later. It's a nice thing and has made us very close.

Ezra and I are praying for you.

Chrissie

Dad's vulnerable side is still in evidence, I'm happy to report, though I do not mean to imply I am happy that he still feels pain sharp enough to bring tears. In addition to learning to cry, by the time Mom died this stoic, stubborn, *nüchtern* German male also had "learned" not to hold back *I love you.*

I thank my mother, for it was through her that these "lessons" were imparted to her knight in shining armor. What a wonderful gift she gave him, gave *us.* Her children have experienced a closeness with our father we hadn't known and always will cherish.

Holding on while letting go

Those who have the strength and the love to sit with a dying patient in the silence that goes beyond words will know that this moment is neither frightening nor painful, but a peaceful cessation of the functioning of the body.

— Elisabeth Kübler-Ross

From: Linda Campanella
Sent: Monday, August 24, 2009 10:17 PM
To: Bobye List
Subject: Enfield update

Hi, Bobye. Your beautiful letter arrived in Enfield today and was opened at our "happy hour" gathering, which today included Mom, Dad, Eric, Paula and me. What a lovely letter! I read it to myself and cried (as everyone but Mom observed); it was not read aloud at the time, but Eric, Paula, and my father have since read it. I wish you had heard what each of us had to say about you and what you mean to our family. Thank you!

It has been a rough week, perhaps especially for my father. We have confronted the reality that Nan is dying from, as opposed to living with, cancer. She does seem to be on a decline. There were moments last week when it seemed she really was on her way out, and perhaps it was at one of those moments that you spoke with my father. He has been on the verge of tears for days. Since you spoke with him, Mom has characteristically rallied a bit. Today was a really good day, as the attached photos perhaps suggest. I have been here since yesterday, having come home a day early from a wonderful (and much needed) family vacation at the cottage in Essex, MA. Clearly the cancer in her brain is beginning to make its presence known in more tangible ways. Mom is profoundly weak, and her mental alertness/clarity is not what it used to be. That said, this morning she and I did two crossword puzzles together! More often than not, though, she is kind of "out of it." If you were to call, you'd surely notice that you are not speaking with the Nan who visited with you on the deck just two weeks ago. It is sad. But she continues to be, as Eric pointed out tonight, an inspiration for reasons you spoke of so lovingly in your letter. We will continue to take things a day at a time, hoping that she will continue to be pain-free and enjoying all the good moments in each day for as many days as she is still with us.

I hope you've had a wonderful month at Wildwood. It of course makes me sad that Mom and Dad did not, after all, make it to the lake last week with the Blakers. Nevertheless, the Blaker visit to the east coast was a big highlight for both Mom and Dad, even if they never made it to the cottage. Paula decided to stay on a while and will be here until Friday afternoon. Eric came to Enfield late this afternoon and will stay through Wednesday morning. I'll head back to West Hartford tomorrow morning and will return Wednesday night. Dad works Thursday and Friday. Life goes on...

We'll give you a call on Thursday or Friday, trying Wildwood first and then Brooklyn. I think I remember correctly that you'll be at the lake through end of August.

Much love from us all,
Linda

P.S. This has been typed in haste and when tired; please excuse typos and other errors! XOX

From: Linda Campanella
Sent: Wednesday, August 26, 2009 10:08 AM
To: Betty Fitzjarrald
Subject: RE: Summer Days

Hi, Aunt Betty. You have been on my mind and either a call or e-mail has been on my "to-do" list. Your e-mail this morning provides a good reminder and impetus. I'm home working and catching up a little today, following a week at Essex and then two days in Enfield. Glad to know things are good with you in Maine. I know already how much you are looking forward to the visit by Lance and Aiden. Enjoy every minute or your time with them.

Things in Enfield are not especially good. It seems clearer to us now that the dying process is underway, I'm afraid. There have been no more outings and, sad to say, I suspect there won't be too many more. A few days before Paula and family arrived (August 16) we were still thinking it possible that Mom would make it to Wildwood for a couple days, or at least a day trip, but unfortunately she did not do well last week (despite truly enjoying the Blakers' visit) and at times had folks thinking she might just go to sleep and stay asleep. The brain cancer seems to be manifesting itself in more tangible ways now. Last week she was very weak, sleepy, cross-eyed at times, and often not too alert. That generally describes her condition. However, yesterday when I was there we had a darn good day, all things considered. We worked on some crossword puzzles together in the morning, for example. I'll attach a few photos taken Monday (including one with dear friend Bev Gray, whom you've heard about) so you see she still looks really good.

But on balance she is clearly declining. She cannot use the walker anymore for transfers from daybed to wheelchair or recliner chair. It is, to be sure, very sad. My father has been especially hard hit by this most recent decline; he has been on the verge of tears much of the past ten days, often choking up a little. Paula decided to stay on a little while longer; her family returned to Washington on Sunday morning, and she will fly back on Friday. It has been great having her here. And Eric continues to visit every week, providing a dose of really good medicine for Dad. Claudia is at Essex this week and early next week with her family but surely will be back in Enfield soon. Dad continues to work a couple/few days a week, which also is good medicine. I'll return to Enfield tonight because he will work Thursday and Friday.

We do not know what lies ahead in terms of either further decline or a timeline, so we continue to take each day as it comes, hoping it will be a relatively good one. Mom does still understand everything, recognizes everyone, interacts in totally appropriate ways, laughs when something funny happens, etc. In other words, she is still with us; it's just that there is less of her left, if you know what I mean. It's hard to explain. And Lord knows it is difficult to watch—especially for Dad, whose heart is really aching these days.

The good news, if you can call it that, is that Mom still is experiencing *no* pain, nor will she, thanks to the medications hospice will make available. I believe she truly believes the promise that there will be no pain for her to endure. On Monday I made her another promise: I told her I would always, always take care of Dad and that she need not worry about him. I know her biggest "fear" about dying is leaving her sweetheart behind, and alone.

I hope (and believe, based on her reaction) that she feels unburdened a little by that fear based on what I thankfully managed to tell her without totally breaking down in tears and bawling. Just the thought of it breaks my heart. It will be so important for Dad, himself, to tell her at some point that she needn't worry, that he will be okay; I think she will need to hear those words from him before she will be able to let go.

I know she would love to hear your voice, as would Dad. Don't hesitate to call—even to speak just with him. Just be prepared that you may be saddened if you speak with Mom. She doesn't sound like the Nan you remember. But you can be sure: On the inside she is still the same incredible, wonderful, strong, loving person she has always been. And that person still shines through in special ways each day, making us grateful she is still with us. But sometimes, and now more often, it seems to me we are being selfish in wanting her to keep living, because her quality of life is no longer very good. On the other hand, she loves her family so much and I know she is happy when she is with us. Her family has always been the most important thing in her life. As Judy Riggs, our friend from Essex, put it to me last week: She (Mom) is not ready to leave the party yet. And two weeks ago, when I was talking with Mom about her situation, she did say that while she is not afraid of dying, she is afraid of missing her family. If only she knew how terribly her family will miss her.

Anyway ... I can't type more because, as you might expect, I have made myself cry (actually, I'm bawling!) by bringing all these thoughts to the surface. Frankly, it is something I probably need to do more, because I keep so much pain buried inside me in an effort to be strong for others (principally Mom and Dad). Sometimes the floodgates just open and the depth of my sorrow pours out. This is one of those moments. I am sorry, but grateful, that you have provided the outlet.

Much love,
Linda

From: Linda Campanella
Sent: Sunday, August 30, 2009 9:16 PM
To: Betty Fitzjarrald
Subject: the journey

Dear Aunt Betty,

The journey seems to be coming to an end. Please keep Mom and Dad in your prayers in the coming days. I will try to find time to call. Am on my way to Enfield now, having just returned from NYC/JFK where we put Steve on a plane to Florence for the semester. Paula is still there. Claudia is en route. Eric is on call and may be on his way. Dad is so, so sad. This afternoon they told each other how much they love each other; it was one of the few things Mom had the energy or ability to do; clearly she still has strength for what is most important.

Love,
Linda

From: Linda Campanella
Sent: Monday, August 31, 2009 4:27 PM
To: Eric Sachsse
Cc: Linda Campanella
Subject: a not-so-happy happy hour

Sad … We are approaching happy hour, but I'm not so happy. It will be my first of so many in Enfield this past year (except for those when she was in the hospital) without Nan joining us. She is present physically but not with us in other ways, if you know what I mean. You and B were here for what probably will prove to be her last "good day." Be glad of that. She has had a few alert, good *moments* today (enough to cheer Dad a bit), but they are few and far between. She was able to eat something and drink something at both breakfast and lunchtime, which is very good; but she really struggles with meds. Soon swallowing a pill is going to be impossible, it seems. The hospice nurse will now make a daily visit. Dad plans to work tomorrow, as I'm sure he will tell you when you next call. He is at the hospital now because he needs to check out some equipment needed for a procedure he is to perform tomorrow. He groused about it as he was leaving an hour ago following a call from a physician, but beneath the surface I believe he was like a kid jumping for joy. *They need me and they want me for something especially challenging. Tomorrow will be fun. Yay!*

XO
LSC

From: Linda Campanella
Sent: Thursday, September 03, 2009 10:47 AM
To: Marjorie Campanella
Subject: FW: Family photo

Hi, Margie and Dom.

My mother is taking the final steps on her journey. Perhaps Joe told you she took a major turn for the worse on Saturday afternoon/evening. The attached Campanella family photo was taken just as her condition began to decline. It was very painful for the boys to say a final good-bye. Sunday was a terrible day in Enfield; Mom was not at all with it and barely awake, struggling to swallow... Monday all four Sachsse children were in Enfield, Eric left yesterday and a heartbroken Paula is on a plane back to Washington state right now, having twice extended her stay. Nan had a few good moments on Monday, including enough to allow her to join us on the deck for the "happy hour" that has become, during this past year, a bit of a tradition (so as to inject living and laughter and some normalcy into her days); the attached photo was taken then, and it shows both her distant look and the heartache in my father's face, especially his eyes.

I believe for a number of reasons that Nan is ready to move on, although she seems to be hanging on, perhaps, as she told me two weeks ago, because she is still afraid she will miss her family; this has been her only fear of dying. On Saturday morning, during an incredibly powerful spiritual moment that I'll tell you about some day, I was, for the first time, ready to let her go because she seemed so totally at peace and enveloped in God's presence and grace. My father is still struggling to let her go, I'm afraid. This long goodbye has been excruciating for him, and to watch her fade away is almost more than he can bear. Please keep him in your prayers.

Love,
Linda

From: Linda Campanella
Sent: Friday, September 04, 2009 4:16 PM
To: Bobye List
Subject:

Bobye, I don't mean to make you cry, but I will. I'd rather tell you this than not, because it reinforces how meaningful *all* your expressions of love and friendship this past year have been…My father just cut one of the yellow roses from your lovely bouquet and put it on my mother, who looks peacefully lovely right now. Yellow roses were *their* roses. It was a beautiful moment, even as hearts were breaking. L

Date: Sun, 6 Sep 2009 21:07:33
From: Linda Campanella
To: Valerie Smith
Subject: Enfield update

Hi, Val. Since Thursday we have been holding vigil by Mom's bedside. She seems unable, or unwilling, to give up the fight she has fought so bravely and graciously this past year—and on September 8 it WILL be a year. Dad has said a number of times that he has no more tears to cry, and then he cries again. The family is together and we are supporting each other. Paula had to fly back to Washington on Thursday and this of course was very difficult; but she is here in spirit.

We are exhausted but, like Mom, at peace with where things are. She is lying peacefully in bed, looking lovely and comfortable. Her breathing is shallow and somewhat strained, but actually better than it was yesterday. There is no pain that we can discern, but she has been given morphine just in case; none of us can imagine that her head does *not* ache, and one of the promises we (and hospice) made her early in all this was that she'd not have any pain. Dad pinned a yellow rose on her shirt yesterday in one of many moving, heartbreaking moments between the two of them.

At this point we are thinking the final good-bye is hours but certainly no more than days away. We now expect the celebration of life gathering will be next Saturday, the 12th.

I am emotionally and physically drained. (So drained that I'm not even sure I haven't already sent you an update!) Believe it or not, my eighty-three-year-old father-in-law, whom I (and our kids) adored, suffered a massive stroke Friday afternoon and died Friday evening at 7:45. Joe made it to the Cape in time to join his mother and sister at Hyannis Hospital before the last breath was taken. So on Friday I was getting text-message updates from Joe and sending my father-in-law my love and goodbye messages via text message just as I was sitting by Mom's bed listening and trying to say comforting, loving things to ease her transition. I was needing and wanting to be in three places at once: with my parents, with my husband, and with my children, who were confronting the terrible, sad reality of losing two dearly loved grandparents at essentially the same time. Too surreal! It is all so, so sad.

We know you are keeping us in your thoughts and prayers and we appreciate this. Your friendship across the miles and over so many years has meant so much to Mom, as I hope you know.

Hugs,
Linda

From: Linda Campanella
To: Bobye List
Sent: Tuesday, September 08, 2009 7:43 AM
Subject: Re: thinking of you

Good morning, Bobye. Thanks for keeping us in your thoughts.

Yes, Mom is still with us this morning; no real change from last night. This does make planning anything difficult. We will want/need to put an obituary in the papers no later than Thursday if there is to be an event on Saturday, so yes: those plans are at the moment tentative, although I need to meet with the caterer today to "finalize" some things. If Nan does not die today I will not go to the funeral for my father-in-law but would expect to attend the burial on Thursday. Joe's family understands. At the moment my father needs my support.

Eric went home yesterday but hopes to return Wednesday evening. Claudia needs to go home for at least 24 hours and probably will leave today, probably returning Thursday. Paula is on pins and needles; not only is our event on Saturday on hold; so too are her airline ticket purchases!

Today is the one-year anniversary of Mom's diagnosis, and it is the first dreary day we have had in almost two weeks. Perhaps this is the day. Dad just sat looking at her and said softly, "Sooner or later she will go away." Then more tears from a reservoir he claimed days ago had been depleted.

So we expect to have another day similar to those we've been experiencing. We did decide to have a hospice nurse come today to take a look at where things stand. I called yesterday just to "talk." It seems we are doing everything "right," but it is so hard. We've been reassured she is not suffering at all. No, she has not taken fluids, food, or meds in quite a few days, and she does not move or speak or interact; she is essentially in a coma.

So sad.

Much love as always,

Linda

From: Linda Campanella
Sent: Wednesday, September 09, 2009 12:37 PM
To: Rev. Gary Miller
Subject: Nancy L. Sachsse (aka Mom)

Gary,

My mother passed away peacefully at noon today. Thank you for your love, support, and prayers.

Linda

From: Rev. Gary Miller
Sent: Wednesday, September 09, 2009 1:06 PM
To: Linda Campanella
Subject: RE: Nancy L. Sachsse (aka Mom)

I leave you now and you have sorrow.
But I will see you again ...
And, the next time ...
Our joy will last forever.

Trust it my friend, for it makes sense of everything else ... even in our most difficult separations.

We love you!

The birds

My mother loved birds, and in the final months before she died, birds assumed a somewhat central place in her life. In the months after her death, birds played an unexpectedly central role in mine.

On one of her visits to Enfield in early spring, Claudia brought three colorful birdfeeders of the sort that was attracting birds by the flock at her home in New Jersey. In Enfield they were situated along the edge of the deck railing so that Mom and Dad could sit on the deck, or look out onto it from the living room, and be visited by a variety of birds attracted to the birdseeds specially selected by Claudia's husband Billy. In time, the deck area established itself as a favorite dining spot for cardinals, blue jays, mourning doves, finches, and tufted titmice. Along with the birdfeeders, Claudia had brought Mom a book that helped us identify birds not only by their appearance but also by their calls. Mom derived much joy from this book and soon thought of at least four friends who might enjoy it equally. On two of my subsequent visits to Enfield, I picked up extra copies Mom had ordered from Barnes & Noble for these bird-watching buddies.

Once Mom became largely confined to her daybed in the living room, Claudia had another wonderful bird-related idea. On one of her visits in the early summer she brought along a bird feeder that could be affixed to a window via suction cups. The head of Mom's daybed was at the window looking out onto the porch, and so the little birdfeeder was placed where she could watch for birds if her head was turned to face out onto the backyard. Before too long, birds were appearing at the window, close enough that we could watch them painstakingly use their beaks to crack the outer shell of seeds in order to reach the tastier kernels inside.

As Mom became weaker and the end appeared to be drawing nearer, Claudia had yet another idea, one that would allow Mom to continue enjoying birds even though she no longer spent time on the deck (except for happy hours, which we did still try to make a daily event) and did not look out the living room window much because when she was lying in bed she was usually asleep. In August, by which time Claudia and I were each spending half a week in Enfield full-time so that Dad would have a helper at all times of the day or night, Claudia arrived one Sunday afternoon with a beautiful antique bird cage (lovely, as all things Claudia procured and gifted always were!) that was home to two precious little zebra finches. These feathered friends—mates, in fact—made sweet, soft sounds that filled the house and warmed Mom's heart whenever she heard or watched them. The cage was periodically brought over to Mom's bed and placed on the adjustable hospital table we were using for most of her meals by this point. Mom would stick her finger through the metal bars of the cage and try to interact with the little creatures. She had named them Tweetie and Twitter, matter-of-factly admitting, not with embarrassment but with a self-effacing smile, that she no longer seemed to have the ability to come up with any more creative or original names.

Even when she had disappeared into a coma, the birds visited Mom's bedside. We so hoped she could hear their muted and cheerful chirping.

Before she had closed her eyes and lost her ability to interact, I asked her what kind of bird she would have been, had she been born a bird. I was already anticipating that, after her death, I would want to feel connected to her whenever I saw that bird. I expected her answer would be that she'd have been a hummingbird, as I believed this to be her favorite bird, although Claudia thought chickadee! Though she heard the question, Mom was not able to prove either of us right, as she was unable to respond. I asked a few times, but I should have asked her a few days earlier. I still believe she'd have answered, "I would like to have been a hummingbird."

When death was near, I found myself whispering in Mom's ear that she should fly off like the birds at her window, fly off to the heavens, release her spirit on the wings of love. She needed, it seemed, to be released; she needed to let go, let go of her irrepressible will to live and love. I am not sure if in these moments of awaiting death and anticipating loss my suggesting the image of a bird flying off was more for her benefit and comfort or, subconsciously, my own.

Before loading her car for the return trip to New Jersey the day after the celebration of Mom's life, Claudia asked Dad if he might like to keep the birdcage and zebra finches as both a physical reminder of Mom and a source of noise and life in a house that would soon be quiet and feel empty. To our surprise, he said he would keep them. But then as the packing up continued that afternoon, he changed his mind, and soon the cage was taken into the garage and joined everything else waiting to be loaded into Claudia's van. Paula and her family had already left for the airport, and Eric, Jen and his girls also had taken off following a whole-family brunch at the Windsor Marriott. My clan was back in West Hartford. Only Claudia's family and I were still in Enfield with Dad.

We gathered in the garage and on the driveway as the final loading up was underway. Suddenly, Dad noticed and announced that one of the zebra finches was missing from the cage, which was still on the garage floor. He bent down to look more closely and reported that one of the little bars of the cage seemed to have fallen out, creating an escape route. We were quite upset about this unexpected loss. The birds had assumed a special significance to us all because of the special role they had played. Dad stood up and started walking toward the shelves in the back of his garage, where he kept some of his tools, saying he would use wire clippers to cut a piece of coat hanger the length of what was needed to close the hole and keep the escaped bird's mate safe. At just that moment, those of us who were still looking at the cage shrieked as the second finch flew the coop, literally, and flew around the garage for a moment before flying outside and swooping around our heads. One of Claudia's sons ran after it, for the little creature did not fly high or fast, and it seemed we might be able to recapture it. But we could not.

We stood on the driveway in stunned silence. In a minute, the silence was broken by Dad, who said in a very soft and sad voice, "I think they have flown away to be with Nan."

He quickly turned around and walked back into the garage to let his tears flow more freely and privately. We all were in tears.

Could there possibly be any explanation more logical, or more moving, than Dad's theory that the zebra finches, their purpose on earth fulfilled, had now flown away to be with the spirit they had helped set free? Were these inseparable lovebirds the earthly embodiment of Nan's spirit? Had we just watched her loving spirit ascend to heaven?

These questions really did occur to me during this somewhat spookily spiritual experience. I was unnerved, but in a beautiful way. These were awesome questions to ponder in a moment of great sadness and loss, because they presented wonderful, indeed wonder-filled, possibilities that were comforting to contemplate. Nan would not be alone; she would have her birds with her. I found especially touching that it was my *nüchtern* (rational) father who had imagined this most unscientific, irrational explanation for the birds' escape.

In the days and weeks following Mom's death, I spotted birds everywhere. I gathered and surrounded myself with birds: a pair of mahogany birds for my bookshelf, a silver pendant, a soapstone hand-carving of a mother bird with baby bird nestled beneath her wing, a colorful mosaic sun catcher for my window with a hummingbird in the center, three hand-carved and hand-painted bird Christmas tree ornaments—a bluejay, cardinal, and chickadee—spotted at the Sugarloaf Crafts Festival (they will be perfect stocking stuffers for my three sons), a bluebird paperweight for Dad, and then one for Eric, coffee mugs for my sisters and me.

October 8, 2009

Dear Eric, Claudia, and Paula,

Yesterday I found three coffee mugs that I couldn't resist buying. Their appeal was not so much their design (though I do like them very much) but rather the idea they planted in my head. I would love for the three of us daughters to be connected with each other, and for all of us to be connected with Mom, every morning when we drink our coffee from mugs decorated with birds, each one a little different. As we all know, Mom loved her coffee, and she loved birds. For me, and perhaps for you, birds have taken on a new significance and special meaning since Mom's death. So I purchased the mugs and am giving one to each of you as an early birthday present to Mom, who unfortunately isn't here to receive our gifts and celebrate with us this year but whose presence and love I'm sure we'll feel anyway. I also have a little present for Eric. This morning I was in an antiques store and came upon a paperweight featuring a bird. I had to buy it. Ten days ago I gave Dad a bird paperweight for his desk. Now you'll both have one. Call me silly or sentimental, but I love the idea of all five of us being connected with each other and with Mom in this way.

Love,
Linda

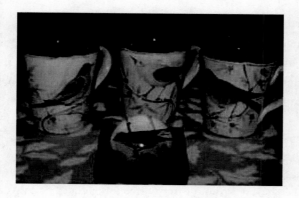

Claudia had similar instincts. We both spent Dad's birthday with him (on October 9, exactly one month after Mom's death), and she had brought me a bird-gift as well: a beautiful hand-painted soap dish and bar of soap wrapped in gift paper matching the design on the dish. She brought Dad a life-size and real-looking bird that now hangs from his chandelier in Enfield; Mom is present with him when he eats his meals alone. Claudia also gave him a little wall-mounted birdcage with two little red bird figures in it.

Never having lost anyone so dear to me as my mother, I never knew how one seeks and clings to anything that keeps us connected with, and helps us feel an abiding presence of, that which no longer exists physically. Today, I see Mom, I feel Mom, I keep loving Mom in these birds. I know that in the spring I will welcome the return of birds in an entirely new way and with far greater anticipation than ever before.

Birds make me think of Mom. When I remember her, she is still with me. That is exactly where I want her to be.

Poetry

One of the things I remember doing soon after getting the news of Mom's diagnosis was visiting a small bookstore in the Center of West Hartford, a shop that somehow manages to survive despite the presence nearby of bookselling behemoths Border's and Barnes & Noble as well as the ubiquitous presence of amazon.com. I asked the proprietress where I would find books on dying and grief, as I figured someone else's wisdom might help me know what I was in for and how I might cope. I found and thumbed through quite a few interesting books but didn't buy any of them. Instead, I bought a book of poetry for Mom: *Good Poems*, selected and introduced by Garrison Keillor of Prairie Home Companion fame. As described on the inside front cover of my edition, it is an extraordinary collection of poems, "chosen by Keillor for their wit, their simplicity, their passion, and their utter clarity in the face of everything else a person has to deal with."[2] The poem "Kaddish," with which I began this book, is borrowed from *Good Poems*; I did not discover it until after my mother's passing, when it resonated with me in ways it wouldn't have, had I found it a year ago.

---

2   Garrison Keillor, ed., *Good Poems*, Selected and Introduced by Garrison Keillor (New York: The Penguin Group, 2002)

I have never loved poetry as much as Mom did, but I predict this may change. It is changing already. I have read a lot of poetry since her death and find myself connecting with it and appreciating it, or its potency, in previously unknown (to me) ways. Ten years or so ago, Mom started sending a few carefully selected poems to all eleven of her grandchildren on a monthly basis. She loved poetry enough to hope her offspring would love it equally—or at least give it a chance! If I ever had trouble thinking of what Mom might enjoy and appreciate as a little gift on her birthday or Mother's Day, I could always (and often did) safely resort to getting her a book of poetry. She kept *Good Poems* within reach on the little table next to the recliner chair in which she passed many hours on many days. She absolutely loved this particular collection, and we sometimes read from it, or from others on her shelves, when we were together on days I spent in Enfield.

The intrinsic and mysterious power of poetry, perhaps especially potent in difficult times ("in the face of everything a person has to deal with"), is apparently well understood by certain people who feel called to engage in "poetry ministry." In much the same way music therapy is thought to have helpful, healing impact, I suppose poetry also is thought to transmit therapeutic benefit when administered (or ministered) effectively. I discovered there are good people who believe good poems can do good. Such people exist within my own faith community, and within weeks of my mother's diagnosis, an envelope filled with a half dozen or so typed and Xeroxed poems arrived in my mailbox on a weekly basis, sent by members of my church's poetry ministry. I had known of this group but confess to never having paid much it attention.

From: Linda Campanella
Sent: Saturday, November 22, 2008 11:08 AM
To: robertpoetry@ ...
Subject: Thank you.

Dear Bob,

Many thanks for the several envelopes you have mailed to me for my mother. What a lovely collection (including one or two of your own verses) you assembled and shared. On one of my visits last week I presented her a three-ring binder with all the poems you have sent; I included a cover page, which I shall cut and paste below, as it includes some quotes that you, as a fellow lover of poetry, may find of interest. I also share here a little Haiku I've come across. It is rather poignant, particularly if one interprets it in the context of a life that will end too soon.

> *The only problem*
> *with Haiku is that you just*
> *get started and then*
> —Roger McGough

In short, Bob, I am very grateful for the poetry ministry at Asylum Hill Congregational Church and in particular for your outreach to me and, through me, to my mother. She appreciated this gesture very much herself; she told me it provides further evidence that I am part of a truly special faith community. Indeed!

She is doing relatively well. Chemo is on hold halfway through the four-course regimen, as it has thrown her for a loop; but the X-ray last week showed that the poison has had some effect in terms of shrinking the growths in her chest, which should encourage her to resume the treatment when she is feeling better. I hope so. Her treatment is, as the oncologist gently reminded us, palliative, not curative, but I will welcome and be grateful for any successful strategy that extends her life, *if* the quality of life is good.

I wish you and your family a very happy Thanksgiving.

With warm regards and sincere appreciation,

Linda

To Mom, who loves poetry
From Linda, who loves you
November 2008

A man should hear a little music, read a little poetry, and see a fine picture every day of his life, in order that worldly cares may not obliterate the sense of the beautiful which God has implanted in the human soul.

—Johann Wolfgang von Goethe

He who draws noble delights from sentiments of poetry is a true poet, though he has never written a line in all his life.

—George Sand, 1851

Poetry is a packsack of invisible keepsakes.

—Carl Sandburg

It is the job of poetry to clean up our word-clogged reality by creating silences around things.

—Stephen Mallarme

Poetry is when an emotion has found its thought and the thought has found words.

—Robert Frost

Poetry is not a turning loose of emotion, but an escape from emotion; it is not the expression of personality, but an escape from personality. But, of course, only those who have personality and emotions know what it means to want to escape from these things.

—T.S. Eliot,
Tradition and the Individual Talent, 1919

Your prayer can be poetry, and poetry can be your prayer.

—Noelani Day

LINDA CAMPANELLA

Everything in creation has its appointed painter or poet and remains in bondage like the princess in the fairy tale 'til its appropriate liberator comes to set it free.

—Ralph Waldo Emerson

We choose our joys and sorrows long before we experience them.

—Kahlil Gibran

Nobody has ever measured, not even poets, how much the human heart can hold.

—Zelda Fitzgerald

After Mom died, I took *Good Poems* from the little table next to her recliner chair and discovered a bookmark (the torn-off top of a receipt from Target dated 9–30–08) wedged between pages 312 and 313. I'm not sure whether it was Chuck Miller's "in celebration of surviving" on page 312 or Donald Hall's "Her Long Illness" on page 313 that struck a chord with Mom; easily either one, or both, could have spoken to her.

in celebration of surviving

when senselessness has pounded you around on the ropes
and you're getting too old to hold out for the future
no work and running out of money,
and then you make a try after something that you know you
won't get
and this long shot comes through on the stretch
in a photo finish of your heart's trepidation
then for a while
even when the chill factor of these prairie winters puts it at
fifty below
you're warm and have that old feeling
of being a comer, though belated
in the crazy game of life

standing in the winter night
emptying the garbage and looking at the stars
you realize that although the odds are fantastically against you
when that single January shooting star
flung its wad in the maw of night
it was yours
and though the years are edged with crime and squalor
that second wind, or twenty-third
is coming strong
and for a time
perhaps a very short time
one lives as though in a golden envelope of light
—By Chuck Miller

Her Long Illness

Daybreak until nightfall,
he sat by his wife at the hospital
while chemotherapy dripped
through the catheter into her heart.
He drank coffee and read
the Globe. He paced, he worked
on poems, he rubbed her back
and read aloud. Overcome with dread,
they wept and affirmed
their love for each other, witlessly,
over and over again.
When it snowed one morning Jane gazed
at the darkness blurred
with flakes. They pushed the IV pump
which she called Igor
slowly past the nurses' pods, as far
as the outside door
so that she could smell the snowy air.
—By Donald Hall

I made a fire one cold October afternoon about a month and a half after Mom died and spent a couple hours with *Good Poems*. I found quite a few poems that touched me as the two above may have touched Mom. On my own bookmark, an index card, I wrote notes reminding myself of the poems I wanted to revisit and share:

- "To My Mother" p. 371 (for Eric)
- "Yesterday" p. 376
- "When My Dead Father Called" p. 381
- "August Third" p. 382
- "My Dad's Wallet" p. 393
- "Dirge without Music" p. 397
- Untitled by Donald Hall p. 398
- "Kaddish" p. 410

These are eight of twenty-two poems in section eighteen of the Keillor collection; the heading for this section is, no surprise perhaps, "The End." The parenthetical "for Eric" was a reminder to me that I should share with my brother this particular poem, a poignant portrayal of unconditional, undying maternal love as expressed through forgiveness.

To My Mother

I was your rebellious son,
do you remember? Sometimes
I wonder if you do remember,
so complete has your forgiveness been.

So complete has your forgiveness been
I wonder sometimes if it did not
precede my wrong, and I erred,
safe found, within your love,

prepared ahead of me, the way home,
or my bed at night, so that almost
I should forgive you, who perhaps
foresaw the worst that I might do,

and forgave before I could act,
causing me to smile now, looking back,
to see how paltry was my worst,
compared to your forgiveness of it

already given. And this, then,
is the vision of that Heaven of which
we have heard, where those who love
each other have forgiven each other,

where, for that, the leaves are green,
the light a music in the air,
and all is unentangled,
and all is undismayed.

—By Wendell Berry

I don't think Mom ever would have characterized Eric as a rebellious son, though there were moments when she could have conferred that distinction on him based on his having done something to earn it (as most teenage boys do). Rebel or not, Eric was Mom's only son, and I know this made their relationship special. This poem made me think of Eric, and our mother, not so much because it was a message from son to mother, but because of its focus on forgiveness. I was reminded of the e-mail Mom had sent to Eric's daughter Clare soon after her diagnosis, a message in which she had written, "Forgiveness is a very big thing. Simply said, I do not want to die needing to forgive anyone or needing to be forgiven by anyone."

May Sarton's poem "August Third" spoke more directly to me as a daughter. The poem, in the voice of an aging woman thinking of her long-gone mother, suggested that even in my own old age, feeling like an "old camel getting to her knees," I will continue to be inspired and guided by the example of my mother's courage during her last year.

August Third

These days
Lifting myself up
Like a heavy weight,
Old camel getting to her knees,
I think of my mother
And the inexhaustible flame
That kept her alive
Until she died.

She knew all about fatigue
And how one pushes it aside
For staking up the lilies
Early in the morning,
The way one pushes it aside
For a friend in need,
For a hungry cat.

Mother, be with me.
Today on your birthday
I am older than you were
When you died
Thirty-five years ago.
Thinking of you
The old camel gets to her knees,
Stands up,
Moves forward slowly
Into the new day.

If you taught me one thing
It was never to fail life.

What was that "inexhaustible flame" that burned inside my mother for one year and one day? I'll never know, but I'll never forget. And thirty-five years from now, if I'm still around, I will still long for my mother to be with me, as the unknown daughter in "August Third" did. My version of her poem, her message to Mother, will be titled "October Twenty-Fourth."

The poems from the poetry ministry at Asylum Hill Church came for many weeks, but I confess that I did not share them all with my mother, and eventually I asked Bob to stop sending them. Before bringing them with me to Enfield I put aside those whose message seemed too dark or stark. I believe Bob may have thought initially that Mom was closer to death than she was; he clearly had not factored in the "inexhaustible flame that kept her alive until she died." Too many of the poems for my liking addressed the topic of death and dying, and this was not the topic we chose to focus on when we believed there was so much more living to do. These verses, all prayerfully selected with the most loving of intentions on the part of Bob and his fellow "ministers," would not have been a source of comfort or inspiration to Mom in the weeks and then months when she "move(d) forward slowly into the new day" with a sense of joyful anticipation of what today, and tomorrow, would bring.

Just days after Mom died, another envelope with Bob's return address on it arrived. It had been many months since I'd seen one of these in the mail. Perhaps because I was so emotionally fragile and in need of comfort—open to it, seeking it, *craving* it—the verses in this last envelope from the poetry ministry penetrated very deeply. Whereas the poems sent in fall of 2008 were intended to minister to my mother's emotional needs, these last selections were meant to minister to those grief-stricken over her death. They were intended to minister to me. From my perspective, admittedly a selfish one now, Bob had saved the best for last, and I quickly sent him a heart-felt, tear-soaked thank-you note telling him exactly that.

The first selection, the seventh stanza of "Memories of My Father" by Galway Kinnell, promises that after we have cried rivers of tears and come to terms with the permanence of physical loss, we will experience the presence, a "million moments of presence," no less, of our lost loved one in truly beautiful ways. I wished fervently to believe this.

> Those we love from the first
> can't be put aside, or forgotten
> after they die, they still must be cried
> out of existence, tears must make
> their erratic runs down the face,
> over the fullnesses, into
> the craters, confirming
> the absent will not be present,
> ever again. Then the lost one
> can fling itself outward, its million
> moments of presence can scatter
> through consciousness freely, like snow
> collected overnight on a spruce bough
> that in mind-morning bursts
> into glittering dust in the sunshine.

The second poem articulated both simply and achingly how desperate we are—I was—to believe death is not the end of a relationship with someone we love and need in our lives. I did not wait for my next visit to Enfield to share this second poem, "Belief" by Ann Thorp, and the Galway Kinnell poem with my father. He needed their reassuring message right away. He was not sure whether or where he would find the strength to go on, to find meaning in his life without his life partner. I promptly scanned the poems and sent them via e-mail attachment, typing "Comforting Words" in the subject line before I pressed "send."

Belief

I have to believe
That you still exist
Somewhere,
That you still love me
Somehow.

I have to believe
That life has meaning
Somehow,
That I am useful here,
Sometimes,
That I make small differences
Somewhere.

I have to believe
That I need to stay here
For sometime,
That all this teaches me
Something,
So that I can meet you again
Somewhere.

—By Ann Thorp

This particular poem seemed to articulate what I knew my father was feeling, hoping, and, in moments of intense grief and aloneness, wanting to believe. He told me he did find comfort in these words, and I believe him. I found a printed copy of the poem propped up on his desk the next time I visited him.

In addition to keeping them visible for quick reference and reassurance, Dad also forwarded both poems to two close friends of his and Mom's, one of whom is a widow whose empathy has continued to be a source of strength to my father in the months since Mom's death. She quickly wrote back to Dad, thanking him for sharing the poems and so openly sharing his emotions; she knew him well enough to recognize that this openness was something new, while also being clear evidence of the depth of his pain. In her reply she wrote that "Belief" expressed what she feels as well, "still after 18 years." She acknowledged that while she often feels lonely, "I never feel alone. Larry is with me." And then she wrote, "I *know* that you will feel the same about never being alone. Nan is always with you."

Some people, myself among them, "have to believe"—we simply *must*, in order to cope with our loss and loneliness—that someone we loved and have lost "still exists somewhere" and "still loves me somehow."

Love, always love

Based upon what I have observed in the three and a half months since Mom's death, my father surely must believe Nan still exists somewhere and still loves him. Perhaps he thinks this was her promise to him, embedded in the words she left in lipstick on the Essex mirror. I know it still hurts like hell, but he seems to be coping with his loss as well as anyone in his shoes could. The where-does-she-get-it strength Mom exhibited in her last year is now reflected in the surprising strength Dad is exhibiting in his first year without her. Her resolve to live, even while dying, is now mirrored in his determination to live, even while grieving a loss he was not sure he could survive. Life goes on. Life is good.

To the extent Dad and the four children may be coping relatively well with our grief, credit is perhaps owed to the one we lost. I believe Mom laid out certain expectations and wishes, maybe even promises, that could serve as reassuring guideposts for us.

"Love, always love": *I will always love you. Keep loving me. Love each other. Love never dies.*

"Don't be sad": *There is so much joy in life. Seek it, find it, revel in it. I want you to be happy. I am happy when you are happy. Please don't stop having happy hour!*

"The highest tribute to the dead is not grief but gratitude." These last words, unlike the others, are not Mom's; they are Thornton

Wilder's words, and they are excerpted from one of the three quotes she selected for inclusion on the memorial card we printed for the celebration of life in her honor.

All that we know about those we have loved and lost
is that they would wish us to remember them
with a more intensified realization of their reality.
What is essential does not die but clarifies.
The highest tribute to the dead
Is not grief but gratitude.

Mom did not want us to mourn her death. She wanted us to live life and love life as much as she did, even in her last year.

In the first days and weeks after Mom's death I suggested rather regularly that Dad come to my house for dinner or that I go there for a quick visit. I didn't want to impose myself on him, understanding that he needed time and space to be alone with his pain, but I really didn't want him to be alone all the time, as I couldn't imagine anything more depressing than that. Initially he did not want to come here and discouraged me from going to Enfield too often. His explanation was simple: "I just have to get through this."

He was leaning into the pain, into the grief; taking his licks, so to speak. "I need to tough it out," he'd say. There was no way to avoid it, and so he wanted to just "do" it and, presumably, get it (or at least the worst of it) over with quickly.

After Mom's death, a couple who lived down the street from my parents enclosed with their sympathy card a copy of "Please Be Gentle: An Afterloss Creed" by Jill Englar. I called to thank them for sharing such an important and helpful piece of wisdom. John had lost his wife seven years ago and, according to his current life partner, Julia, he wondered at the time if he "would ever be whole again." The sense of emptiness was overwhelming for him. The creed, along with two years with a bereavement support group, helped John come to terms with his loss. I think the creed, and with

LINDA CAMPANELLA

it John's empathy, helped my father understand the emptiness he felt was both expected and "allowed," and that he was not alone, despite the loneliness he felt.

> *Please be gentle with me, for I am grieving. The sea I swim in is a lonely one and the shore seems miles away. Waves of despair numb my soul as I struggle through each day.*
>
> *My heart is heavy with sorrow. I want to shout and scream and repeatedly ask "Why?" At times, my grief overwhelms me and I weep bitterly, so great is my loss.*
>
> *Please don't turn away from me or tell me to move on with my life or I should be over it by now. I must embrace my pain before I can begin to heal. Companion me through tears and sit with me in loving silence. Honor where I am in my journey, not where you think I should be.*
>
> *Listen patiently to my story. I may need to tell it over and over and over again. It's how I begin to grasp the enormity of my loss. Nurture me through weeks, months and the years ahead as I begin my life long journey. Forgive me when I seem distant and inconsolable. A small flame still burns within my heart and shared memories may trigger both laughter and tears. I need your support and understanding. There is no right or wrong way to grieve. I must find my own path. Please will you walk beside me?*

Julia told me, and I believe, that one does not get over the pain, but one gets *through* it. How one gets through it again is a uniquely personal thing, as the creed suggests.

I did pop in to see Dad very regularly in the first days and weeks and was welcomed, not just by him but also by Muffet, who clearly felt something was upside down or out of kilter in her little world as well. Dad always had a pile of the latest sympathy cards on the dining table for me to read, and we shared some tears over quite a few touching messages. I brought him thank-you note cards to use in acknowledging the many memorial contributions made in Mom's honor and other expressions of kindness and sympathy that he received and appreciated.

He gave me things from the cupboards to take home, saying "I'm never going to eat this stuff. Please. Take it." We played Rummy. I did laundry. He asked me how to use the oven. I spritzed a little Chanel No. 5 on Mom's pillow, as she had asked all her children to do occasionally after she was gone so that Dad could sleep with her memory.

It was a relief and comfort to us all that Dad was plugged back into the work rotation at the hospital immediately. Even in the first week of his widowhood he enjoyed personal contact and professional fulfillment in an environment where he felt both needed and loved. On those work days during the first few weeks I also popped in, even though he was not home. I took care of Muffet and a few other things–like emptying the fridge of things that either were Mom's (for example, all the plain yogurts Dad would never eat) or were going bad. I refreshed the many bouquets of yellow roses that filled the house, first throwing away the wilted ones and then eventually throwing them away altogether. I found some very pretty, real-looking-but-fake yellow roses at a nearby gift shop and put one in a bud vase on his desk, next to a darling picture of the two of them taken in Vienna a few years ago.

I arranged three more, with long stems, in a vase on Mom's bureau, next to another picture of the two of them that sits next to the wood clock housing the urn with Mom's ashes. After asking all his children for input, Dad had picked this beautiful clock from among the many urn options in a catalog provided by the funeral home. Burial will occur at some point in the future, when there are two urns to bury side by side. *Bleib bei mir.*

When I called the hospice spiritual counselor a few weeks ago to ask her for a copy of the poem she read twice to Mom, once when they first met and then again as Mom was at death's door, Faith shared another poem with me. It was beautiful and struck me as being one I might like shared at my own memorial service; just as Mom chose comforting messages (perhaps even requests or instructions) for those who mourned her loss, I might choose this poem as my message to and my wish for those whom I'll leave behind:

When I die if you need to weep
Cry for your brother or sister
Walking the street beside you
And when you need me put your arms around anyone
And give them what you need to give me.

I want to leave you something
Something better than words or sounds.

Look for me in the people I've known or loved
And if you cannot give me away
At least let me live in your eyes and not on your mind.

You can love me most by letting hands touch hands
By letting bodies touch bodies
And by letting go of children that need to be free.

Love doesn't die, people do
So when all that's left of me is love
Give me away.

—Anonymous

I have no doubt that if Mom had encountered this poem[3] in life she would have wanted to share it at the time of her death so we would hear and heed its message. As I read the poem today, I hear Mom's voice, for surely this poem is the unabridged version of her "Love, always love" message to us. She wanted us to know that we would—and should—continue to love her by loving others. Her love for us would never die. We would have to give away (let go of) her body, but her love didn't, and wouldn't, die.

---

3   Elizabeth Roberts and Elias Amidon, eds., *LIFE PRAYERS: From Around the World, 365 Prayers, Blessings, and Affirmations to Celebrate the Human Journey*, (San Francisco: HarperSanFrancisco, 1996), 346

Her life over, all that is left of Mom now is love, the love we shared. But love is also what Mom was made of when she lived. She embodied and exuded love. She gave it away freely and unconditionally, on a whim, just because she felt like it, as she did in an e-mail to my sons one Sunday in March of 2006, for example:

From: Eckart Sachsse
Sent: Sunday, March 12, 2006 8:22 AM
To: Steve Campanella; Phil Campanella; Paul Campanella
Subject: hi from nan

I love you guys, all three of you. You can't possibly know how much. Sorry to be mushy, but sometimes........

THE TRUTH MUST BE TOLD.
THE FACTS MUST BE LAID OUT.
xoxoxo Nan

From: Phil Campanella
To: 'Eckart Sachsse'
Cc: Linda Campanella
Sent: Wednesday, March 15, 2006 8:55 PM
Subject: RE: hi from nan

You are absolutely right, the truth must be told. Thank you for so pleasantly reminding me how much you care about me. I feel the same way about you in return, although I never say it enough. You never know but somebody you really care about could be gone the next day, without your ever getting to say goodbye or tell them how much you love them. Whether it's your brother, sister, dog, grandparent, parent, it's always good to tell them how much you love them, even if it is "mushy."
     Thanks again for caring,
     Phil

From: Eckart Sachsse
Sent: Thursday, March 16, 2006 5:15 PM
To: Phil Campanella
Cc: Linda Campanella
Subject: Re: hi from nan

Hi! Thanks for your reply...you didn't have to! You're right, we don't tell people often enough that we love them, But...then again...we can't just go 'round with mushy "I love yous" all the time. Once in awhile comes the urge to blurt it out, though...and that was the urge I had. Some people will *never* have that urge...Opa is a good example. Yet he cares and loves so much! In the end, I suppose, actions still speak louder than words. And yes, I do...
    ...love you! Nan

Can one ever say *I love you* too often? Probably not. But surely we can be stingy with our emotions, and too many of us do not say *I love you* nearly often enough. Mom was not one of those people, and her loving is her legacy.

I will be eternally grateful that my mother died knowing how much *she* was loved. As torturous as it was for us to know we would lose her too soon, we had a chance to show and share our love before she died; her eulogy was delivered in life, not death. Too many people regret waiting until after someone is gone to say all the wonderful things they felt about that person.

The *CareNotes* booklet I received from my church after Mom's death ends on a positive note, offering counsel that I think is both encouraging and wise.

When we lose our mothers, we lose much that can't be replaced. But we are also left with much to cherish—memories, unique personality traits and strengths, wisdom, and hopefully an example that can inspire us to offer nurturing love to those who remain in our lives. A mother's love, after all, is never lost if it is passed on.

In grieving what was lost, I am clinging to what is left. If all that remains of Mom now is love that will not die, that is so very much! And we must give it away, understanding that in giving it away, we also keep it. Her love—*she*—lives in our hearts.

I have seen Mom's love in Dad's heart. It's almost as though the essence of Mom's love has found a new home, a new vessel. I could not possibly describe what I see and feel, but it is real. My siblings agree. His sister in faraway Munich agrees; in a recent conversation with me, she observed that he seems to have become more *zugänglich* (open, accessible, vulnerable). There has been a transformation of sorts. Of the most wonderful sort. This *nüchtern* man, who always was more comfortable with a handshake for his grandkids than a hug, has not turned mushy, by any stretch of the imagination. However, he is no longer stingy with the *I love yous* or even with the hugs.

My father has done all kinds of uncharacteristically loving things in the weeks, now months, since losing his sweetie pie, the "better half" who, in their marriage and family arrangement, was the one "in charge" of the love stuff while he took care of other responsibilities. After all, she was so good at it. A natural. But now she is gone. Who is in charge of love now?

He may not realize it, but he is learning how to do things and assuming roles that go far beyond all the household tasks he never needed to concern himself with when she was in charge (of the house as well as love). As her death approached, he learned how to cry. As his life without her begins, I believe he is learning how to love in a different way. *Her* way.

I see and feel a new warmth in Dad, and in my eyes the source of this warmth is the flame of Mom's loving spirit burning brightly in his heart.

> *Look for me in the people I've known or loved*
> *And if you cannot give me away*
> *At least let me live in your eyes and not on your mind.*
> *You can love me most by letting hands touch hands…*

Love, always love.

October twenty-fourth

From: Linda Campanella
Sent: Monday, October 19, 2009 1:54 PM
To: Valerie Smith
Subject: RE: Good wishes

Hi, Val. I'm sure my father appreciated your taking the time to write to him and to share some memories of Nan. He is doing pretty well, but each expression of sympathy, kindness and/or friendship continues to touch him deeply. The human contact also is comforting.

I think you are right that the week leading up to Mom's birthday is tough. Today I am finding myself quite depressed for the first time. Can't quite put my finger on what or why, but I feel, in a word, lousy. Unable to concentrate or get anything done. Perhaps it's that she won't be here to celebrate her 75th birthday on the 24th. Or it's because in cleaning out my clogged e-mail account this morning I came upon, and dared open, a couple e-mails she sent me this past year; I could hear her voice, and her absence in my life seemed so much more palpable. It hurts that she is no longer on the other end of my daily calls or e-mails. Or perhaps I'm down because I know my father is so lonely. Maybe it's all these things. But so it goes ... We are doing fine and will continue to heal a little bit each day.

Thanks for copying me on your "good wishes" to my dad. Mom's friends have been so good about reaching out to him, and he has been so receptive and grateful.

Best greetings to you,
Linda

From: Linda Campanella
Sent: Monday, October 26, 2009 6:12 PM
To: Bobye List
Subject: your voice-mail

Hi, Bobye. Thanks for your Saturday voice-mail.

You guessed right: We (some of us, anyway) were together to "celebrate" Nan's birthday. There was much more emphasis on "together" than on "birthday" or "celebrate." It just felt necessary—and wise—to not let Dad be alone, so a getaway to the lake was planned. He didn't hesitate for a moment! Joe and I, as well as Eric and B, joined Dad for the weekend, and it was, on the whole, a really nice time—for all.

It was great to be together. We ate well, played games, built fires, and had a "usual" Wildwood weekend ... but for the fact that someone who *usually* is in the cottage with us wasn't. That sad reality was never far beneath the surface of our experience, but we dealt with it. We toasted Mom at "happy hour," and we lit a candle during what would have been her birthday dinner. We included her in our conversation in affirming and loving, not morbid or depressing, ways. I think Eric and I, and also our father, are doing a reasonably good job "letting go" (in grief parlance); this doesn't suggest any of us isn't grieving or missing her terribly. We seem to be working through our pain, managing to find comfort in the knowledge that in many ways Mom is still with us and the bond of love remains (and might even be continuing to strengthen).

We all still have our moments—and I had one sitting by the fire Saturday night, set off by having seen Mom's handwriting on sheets of paper used the last time a certain game had been played with a gang at Wildwood. Claudia is, in general, having quite a tough time of it; Dad senses it and she admits it. And Paula is up to her eyeballs (or higher!) getting ready to uproot her family in the next days and move to Seoul; she has had very few moments in which a wandering mind would wander to anything other than to-do lists! She may hit bottom when she has time and space to let her mind wander freely. For now she seems to be coping—with a lot/ everything!

I started working on a "book" today. I put "book" in quotation marks because I'm not sure what, if anything, will come of this adventure. But I am pursuing it anyway. Eric suggested some time ago that I write a book. For cathartic purposes I am going to try to collect some thoughts based on my experiences. A major focus will be on "living while dying," as this was my major focus during Mom's illness (and the focus of Eric's suggestion). I found an e-mail today that I had written to my siblings two days after the diagnosis; I in effect had made a promise to myself, following some sort of epiphany after 48 hours of intense grief. I wrote, ... *So I will focus on the living still to do, not on the dying that we now know is coming much sooner than we ever imagined. I will concentrate on and believe in the possibility that treatments are going to be very effective in helping her feel good and extending her life so that there will be many happy memories to come in the months and maybe even years to come. I will believe in the power of positive thinking and will invest my energy in willing her to live long and helping her, and Dad, live life as close to "normal" as possible. I will help the sun break through on cloudy days.*

Revisiting the positive parts of the past year will be a key part of my grieving process, it seems. I have to admit, Bobye—and now the tears are coming—that in re-reading what I wrote on Sept. 10, 2008, I do believe I kept my promise to myself (which in many ways, I suppose, also was a promise to my mother). What I wrote from that place of gut-wrenching grief actually did become my *modus operandi* until Sept.

9, 2009. I am pleased and relieved that I managed to do a pretty darn good job. But in doing so, I also buried and hid so much pain. It finally erupted in Enfield in a major meltdown/breakdown (that my father and Eric understood completely) a couple days before she died, and it continues to eke out. My mother, amazingly, remained strong to the end; no meltdown. I will never understand how she managed this; the only explanation I can conjure is a deeply spiritual one.

Sorry to ramble on . . . but I know you understand why I find myself doing so. This, too, is part of my grieving. I need to share. That seems quite obvious!

Hope all's well with you.

Love,

Linda

Linda Campanella

Final thoughts

Though time is getting short (today is December 17), there is still a chance I will have finished writing the first draft of this "book" in time to give a manuscript to my father for Christmas. I am working toward this goal. At the same time, though, I find myself wanting to *not* be finished writing. When I write about my mother, we are together again in some non-corporeal dimension, and I do not want this very real and comforting, if intangible, way of connecting with her to end.

This feeling, this need to keep holding on, makes my thoughts shift to my toes. Much as I don't want my writing about Mom to end, I have not wanted the nail polish on my toes to disappear. Even though at least half of each toenail has no polish on it now (some have none left at all), I am not removing what little remains. What is left was applied one afternoon in early August. I gave Mom a pedicure and then painted my own toes while we lounged together and soaked up some sunshine on her back porch, waiting for Dad to come home and join us for another happy hour. The nails have grown since then, and I've periodically had to cut off their tips and with them some of the polish that connects me with my mother. Silly as it may sound, I don't want the polish to go away. Good thing toe nails grow so slowly.

In writing about Mom and our last year together, I have been rather surprised that my memory of so many details remains so vivid. As a fifty-one-year-old, menopausal woman, I am in the demographic targeted for advertisements touting the memory-enhancing benefits of ginkgo and other herbal supplements. There are many things I cannot remember to save my life, and yet I don't think I have forgotten much at all about the period between day of diagnosis and moment of death. The intensity of my memories must reflect the intensity of the experience itself and the intensity of my emotional investment.

So much of what I've written centers on my intentional focus during that year and a day on life and living rather than death and dying. In reflecting on my obvious, perhaps obsessive, aversion to talk about or anticipate the inevitable, and recalling the many ways in which I tried to ensure Mom would remain hopeful and keep planning things we could write on her calendar, I have had to acknowledge a regret. In trying so hard to avoid talking about her death, I also avoided talking with her about her life.

She didn't seem to *need* to talk about her life *in hindsight*, in open acknowledgment it would be ending soon. (About the closest she came to doing so was when she gave me the packet of things she had saved for her children so we would know how beautiful our parents' love story had been.) And I did not *want* to talk about her life as though it were history; I knew she was going to die, but in those precious moments of togetherness she was still living. Her life's history was still being written, and new memories could still be created.

While avoiding the topic (or anticipation) of death, I did not ask my mother things about her life, interesting or important questions I will never be able to ask her now that she is gone. And this is what I regret. I regret it considerably. There is much I would have enjoyed hearing and appreciated learning if she had been allowed or encouraged to look back instead of forward.

In anticipating her death during our last year together, I think the best I could do, or the most I would permit myself to imagine, was an event, *not* a permanent state: death as the cessation of her life, not as the end of a relationship that had defined and given shape to my own life. I had indulged those thoughts in the first, terrible weeks after her diagnosis, a time when I began immediately to grieve Mom's loss and the end of my relationship with her. But then I purposely and forcefully reined in the grief and resolved to "not go there." From that point on I quite successfully suppressed thoughts about becoming motherless, about all the things that would never happen, about all the things that would never be the same.

In the days following Mom's death, my grief manifested itself not in buckets of tears but in a strange feeling that something just wasn't right, the sensation that something was wrong in my world, something out of place, something amiss. I was keenly aware of feeling an emptiness—the void she left in a life inextricably and intricately linked with hers. I rather quickly came to terms with the reality that Mom had died; this I could make sense of and accept. More difficult to make sense of, and far more challenging to accept as the new reality of my existence, was the permanence, the forever-ness of my loss.

The initial feeling that something was amiss led me to anticipate a moment when things would be right again. Amiss is a temporary state. If something is out of place, we can restore it to its original position. I needed to come to grips with the fact that the void would not be filled again; the sense of something being wrong in my world represented how my world would be from this point forward. My mother was gone and not coming back. I was, *in fact*, motherless.

I did some reading about the "letting go" process when it became clear that one of us might be struggling much more strenuously than the others with the loss of our mother. I wanted to find something potentially helpful to share, although I was cautious about sending anything that might be interpreted as "advice" or misinterpreted as suggesting I believed there was a right way, or a right time, to "let go." I already had read enough to know there is neither. In my search (ever the *Googler!*), I did find, and eventually shared, a few nuggets of what I thought represented wisdom, among them the paragraphs that follow below.

Sometimes, for fear of "letting go," we may find ourselves "holding on" to our pain as a way of remembering those we love. Letting go of what used to be is not an act of disloyalty, and it does not mean forgetting our loved ones who have died.

Letting go means leaving behind the sorrow and pain of grief and choosing to go on, taking with us only those memories and experiences that enhance our ability to grow and expand our capacity for happiness.

We can soothe our pain by thinking of happy memories. The happiness we experienced with our loved ones belongs to us forever.

Death ends a life, but it does not end the relationship we have with our loved ones who have died. The bonds of love are never severed by death, and the love we shared will never die either.[4]

It has been helpful, for me anyway, to remember that "the bonds of love are never severed by death, and the love we share will never die either." But if truth be told, beneath my confident, composed exterior I am an easily distracted, discombobulated daughter just wishing her mom were still here. The world is not right without her in it. Something is still amiss. And I miss her every day in many ways.

Next week is Christmas. She is supposed to be here. I have never *not* had a mother to buy presents for, to drink eggnog with, to show my decorated tree to, to kiss good-bye on Christmas Eve following the traditional dinner with my parents and gift exchange at my house. Her absence, in a word, stinks.

I accept, but I do not *approve*, my new reality. Edna St. Vincent Millay captured this defiant, melancholy feeling beautifully in "Dirge without Music," another poem that made a lasting impression when I read through Garrison Keillor's now dog-eared collection *Good Poems.*

---

4   Marty Tousley, "Grief Healing: Remembering Our Loved Ones on Valentine's Day," published in the January-February 2010 newsletter of The Compassionate Friends Seattle-King County Chapter (Seattle, 2010)

Dirge without Music

I am not resigned to the shutting away of loving hearts in the
        hard ground.
So it is, and so it will be, for so it has been, time out of mind.
Into the darkness they go, the wise and the lovely. Crowned
With lilies and with laurel they go, but I am not resigned.

Lovers and thinkers, into the earth with you.
Be one with the dull, the indiscriminate dust.
A fragment of what you felt, of what you knew,
A formula, a phrase remains,—but the best is lost.

The answers quick and keen, the honest look, the laughter,
        the love,—
They are gone. They are gone to feed the roses. Elegant and
        curled
Is the blossom. Fragrant is the blossom. I know. But I do not
        approve.
More precious was the light in your eyes than all the roses in
        the world.

Down, down, down into the darkness of the grave
Gently they go, the beautiful, the tender, the kind,
Quietly they go, the intelligent, the witty, the brave.
I know. But I do not approve. And I am not resigned.
                                —Edna St. Vincent Millay

The poem captures not only my feelings but also, if I might opine
with obvious prejudice, my mother's essence. Perhaps Millay was
writing about many different people, but my mother was, singularly,
all those things. She was wise and lovely. She was honest, beautiful,
tender, kind, intelligent, witty, brave … so, so brave. Her laughter
and the light in her eyes, especially when she was with the family she
adored, were insignias of her life. Above all, my mother had a loving

heart. She had so much love still to give. Her light was extinguished too soon. And I most assuredly do not approve.

Christmas Eve will be different this year. I could not bear to "celebrate" it at my house with Dad alone. Mom's absence would be painfully palpable. I don't think any of us is ready for that just yet. The scab on the wound is not thick enough. Dad will be well taken care of and entertained by Eric, Jen, and his girls in New Hampshire. This feels right in so many ways. Joe, our sons and I will be spending Christmas with my newly widowed mother-in-law. Like my dad, she will be experiencing her first Christmas without her beloved spouse. Unlike my dad, she had no time to anticipate or begin preparing emotionally to be alone; Dom died less than six hours after his massive stroke on September 4, and Margie is still quite undone by her grief.

Is it better to lose someone suddenly and unexpectedly than to lose him or her after a long illness one knows is terminal? That's a question so many have wrestled with, probably because there is no answer. (Can one option be better when they are both so awful? Are there degrees of terrible?)

I think in my mother's case, it was good, if not better, to have had the time we had with her after her diagnosis. Not everyone is as brave as she was. Through her courage, her love, her grace, and her joyful resolve to keep living and loving, she made the unbearable bearable for us.

As difficult as the long good-bye was, I believe all of us appreciate that there *was* a good-bye, and that we were able, in the months leading up to good-bye, to return some small measure of the immense and intense love Mom had showered on us in her lifetime. We are all grateful to have had a chance to leave nothing unsaid. We are grateful she knew how much she was loved and would be missed. We, her children, are grateful for the chance to have borne witness to the deep love between our parents, never more evident to us than in the final chapter of the love story they both loved to tell. We are grateful to have had the chance to give Mom, as one of my friends put it, "a

Linda Campanella

good death." We are grateful for the many magical moments and all the happy hours. We are grateful for the gift of giving and for all the gifts Mom gave us, in life and also in death. We are grateful to have seen and experienced so much goodness in people—caregivers and friends—who embraced us on our difficult journey.

I recall now the night in January when I fell asleep subconsciously uttering the word "grateful" over and over again, perhaps unknowingly praying in those moments between wakefulness and sleep. At the time I was feeling overjoyed and overcome with gratitude that radiation therapy had done so much good in Mom's brain, buying her more time on earth with the family she was not ready to leave. Now, even in my grief, I find myself grateful for so many things.

Perhaps this is yet more evidence that Mom's loving heart will continue to beat in us. Perhaps it suggests I am doing just as Mom was hoping when she chose Thornton Wilder's words for her memorial card: *The highest tribute to the dead is not grief but gratitude.*

Thank you, Mom. For everything.

And Merry Christmas. I will miss you. I *do* miss you.

Bleib bei mir.

Post script

> **W**HY were the saints, saints? Because they were cheerful when it was difficult to be cheerful, patient when it was difficult to be patient; and because they pushed on when they wanted to stand still, and kept silent when they wanted to talk, and were agreeable when they wanted to be disagreeable. That was all.
>
> It was quite simple and always will be.

After her death I found this card, yellowed from age and obviously cut out from something bigger, in Mom's desk upstairs. Over the years she gathered (and sometimes posted) favorite quotes, verses and words of wisdom that we presume were "notes to self" intended to serve in some way as inspiration and guideposts along her life's journey. Clearly they did.

Nancy L. (Wallwork) Sachsse, 74, of Enfield, CT, passed away on Wednesday, September 9, 2009, at her home with her family by her side. Born on October 24, 1934, in North Andover, MA, she was the daughter of the late Dr. David W. and Louise (Bonney) Wallwork. She lived in Longmeadow, MA, from 1962 to 2006 and was a resident of Enfield since October 2006.

She was a devoted homemaker, wife, mother, grandmother, and friend. A graduate of Wellesley College, where she majored in French, she also studied at the Sorbonne in Paris, France. In 1951, she was one of only twenty high school students nationwide to spend the summer in Europe under the auspices of the American Field Service study abroad program that sponsored students from the U.S. to live with families in foreign countries. In the summer of 1953, she returned to Belgium to interview student candidates for the A.F.S. program of study in the U.S. She later taught French at the former Woodbury High School in Salem, NH. Though it might have been predicted she would marry a Frenchman, in 1956 she fell hopelessly in love with a young German doctor who was doing his residency in the States. She quickly became a student of the German language, which she mastered with ease. She was a lifetime member of the Baystate Medical Center Auxiliary and a member of the Wellesley Club of Greater Springfield.

We knew her as Nan, Nana, Mom, The Missah, and liebe Nancy. She will be remembered for many gifts but perhaps especially for her love of family and friends, her grace and graciousness, her generous spirit, her kindness and empathy, her intelligence and curious mind, her *joie de vivre*. She loved language, books, poetry, history, classical music, foreign films, the Red Sox, a good game of Hearts, a bargain, and sweet corn in August. She also loved yellow roses, her dog Muffet, phone calls and e-mails from her grandchildren, sunsets over the lake in Tolland, watching the boats cruise by and the tide come and go from the porch in Essex, birds in her birdfeeders, rum

Linda Campanella

raisin ice cream, taking photos to record the joy she found in family gatherings of any kind, any time, anywhere. She loved the music of French chanteuse Edith Piaf, whose famous "Non, je ne regrette rien" would be a fitting epitaph for Nan. She loved laughter, and her sense of humor and good spirits buoyed her while giving strength to family and friends during her difficult illness. She loved her friends, near and far, old and new, from Oak Grove to Robbins Island to Morningside Drive to Lakeside Drive at Wildwood to Autumn Fields. More than anything, she adored her husband and sweetheart, with whom it was love at first sight on the day they met on the wharf in the summer of 1956; her four children, whom she taught through example to love unconditionally and abundantly; and her eleven grandchildren, whose various talents and triumphs along life's journey were always a source of great happiness and pride.

She leaves to cherish her memory her beloved husband of 52 years, Eckart Sachsse, M.D., former chairman of the department of radiology at Baystate Medical Center; her four children and their spouses: Linda and Joe Campanella of West Hartford, CT; Eric Sachsse of Hanover, NH; Claudia and Bill Barr of Martinsville, NJ; Paula and Scott Blaker of Ferndale, WA; and her grandchildren: Paul, Steven, and Philip Campanella; Clare, Eva, and Elizabeth Sachsse; Brian and Eric Barr; Zachary, Emily, and Isabelle Blaker; former daughter-in-law Mary Magavern Sachsse; sister-in-law Sophia Sachsse of Munich, Germany; and Betty Fitzjarrald of Maine, whom she loved as a sister. Her family is deeply grateful to the physicians, nurses and other caregivers who helped Nan on her difficult journey with a wonderful combination of competence and compassion. Special and heartfelt appreciation is extended to Dr. Darren O'Neill and to the hospice team at Home and Community Health Services of Enfield. Family and friends are invited to gather at the Hilton Garden Inn, 800 W. Columbus Ave., Springfield, MA, between 12:00 and 3:00 p.m. on Saturday, September 12, for a memorial reception and luncheon in celebration of Nan's life. A private burial service will be at the convenience of the family.

PERMISSIONS AND ACKNOWLEDGMENTS

Wendell Berry, "To My Mother." Copyright © 1997 by Wendell Berry from *The Selected Poems of Wendell Berry*. Reprinted by permission of Counterpoint.

Peggy Heinzmann Ekerdt, "Losing Your Mom." Reprinted by permission of the publisher, Abbey Press, from its line of *CareNotes* booklet series.

Jill Englar, "An Afterloss Creed." Copyright © by Jill Englar. Reprinted by permission of the author.

Donald Hall, "Her Long Illness" from *Without* by Donald Hall. Copyright © 1988 by Donald Hall. Reprinted by permission of Houghton Mifflin Harcourt Publishing Company. All rights reserved.

David Ignatow, "Kaddish" from *Against the Evidence: Selected Poems 1934-1994* © 1993 by David Ignatow. Reprinted by permission of Wesleyan University Press.

Galway Kinnell, "Memories of My Father" from *When One Has Lived a Long Time Alone* by Galway Kinnell, copyright © 1998 by

Galway Kinnell. Used by permission of Alfred A. Knopf, a division of Random House, Inc.

Roger McGough, "Haiku" from *Waving at Trains* by Roger McGough. Copyright © 1992 by Roger McGough. Printed by permission of United Agents (www.unitedagents.co.uk) on behalf of Roger McGough.

Edna St. Vincent Millay, "Dirge without Music." Copyright © 1928, 1955 by Edna St. Vincent Millay and Norma Millay Ellis. Reprinted by permission of Holly Peppe, Literary Executor, The Millay Society.

Chuck Miller, "in celebration of surviving" from *Northern Fields: New & Selected Poems* by Chuck Miller. Copyright © 1994 by Chuck Miller. Reprinted by permission of the author.

Lew Sarett. From *Dealing Creatively with Death: A Manual of Death Education and Simple Burial* by Ernest Morgan and published by Upper Access Books. Copyright © 2001 by Ernest Morgan.

May Sarton, "August Third" from *New and Uncollected Earlier Poems* by May Sarton. Copyright © 1988 by May Sarton. Used by permission of W. W. Norton & Company, Inc.